SHOTLEY PENINSULA

The making of a unique Suffolk landscape

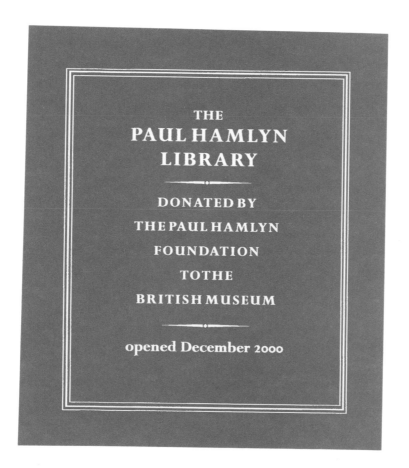

SHOTLEY PENINSULA

The making of a unique Suffolk landscape

SYLVIA LAVERTON

TEMPUS

First published 2001

PUBLISHED IN THE UNITED KINGDOM BY:

Tempus Publishing Ltd
The Mill, Brimscombe Port
Stroud, Gloucestershire GL5 2QG
www.tempus-publishing.com

PUBLISHED IN THE UNITED STATES OF AMERICA BY:

Tempus Publishing Inc.
2 Cumberland Street
Charleston, SC 29401
1-888-313-2665
www.arcadiapublishing.com

Tempus books are available in France and Germany
from the following addresses:

Tempus Publishing Group   Tempus Publishing Group
21 Avenue de la République   Gustav-Adolf-Straße 3
37300 Joué-lès-Tours   99084 Erfurt
FRANCE   GERMANY

British Library Cataloguing in Publication Data.
A catalogue record for this book is available from the British Library.

ISBN 0 7524 1937 4

Typesetting and origination by Tempus Publishing.
PRINTED AND BOUND IN GREAT BRITAIN

Contents

List of illustrations

Acknowledgements

I am most grateful to Suffolk County Council's Archaeological Service for giving me free access to the Sites and Monuments Records, and especially to Dr Colin Pendleton, SMR Officer, for providing maps and drawing, copies of aerial photographs and detailed data on individual sites in the peninsula. He and his colleagues John Newman, Edward Martin and Judith Plouviez have read and commented critically on the text as it evolved, saving me from gross errors of fact and judgement on archaeological matters. Documentary research has supported Professor Harper-Bill's suggestion that Torintuna's DB church could have been a minster. Place-name aspects have been vetted by Dr Margaret Gelling whose support and advice I much appreciate. I am also indebted to Dr Gillian Fellows-Jensen for reading the chapter on Danish influence in the peninsula and for contributing an analysis of Domesday Book personal-names. Also to Dr Barbara Crawford for her comments on the significance of the dedication to St Clement of Harkstead's lost chapel. Sincere thanks are due to the peninsular landowners who granted access to their fields and to all those enthusiasts who shared field-walking expeditions. The Suffolk Record Office staff never failed to produce the many documents needed. The County Library Service has been invaluable, providing access to essential written sources not held in Suffolk. I also thank the Ipswich Metal Detectors Club for lending me their Shotley findspot maps, Derek Palmer for details of his metalwork finds, Brian Newton (SCC Countryside Service) for supplying footpath maps, Hazel Hicks who made all the line drawings, and Sharward Services for typing. Robert Markham advised on geological matters; Norman Scarfe on historical problems. Copyright sources are acknowledged in the text and illustrations.

Many friends in the Shotley Peninsula have provided local knowledge. Richard Pipe's long-term interest in my researches, his readiness to share his considerable knowledge of south-east Suffolk and, not least, his ability to criticise with kindness, have been invaluable. When the late Gwen Dyke was collecting the Deben Valley place-names she suggested that I might attempt to do the same for the Shotley Peninsula. This book, though not quite what she had in mind, is dedicated to her memory.

Foreword

It is rare for an individual to combine a detailed place-name study of an area with a thorough survey of all available archaeological sources, to produce a comprehensive account of settlement patterns, land-use and communications. That Sylvia Laverton has achieved this notable feat for the Shotley Peninsula in south-east Suffolk demonstrates above all that systematic and thorough local archaeological and place-name research is alive and well with the consequent results laid out in this book. Building on her previous place-name work on Woolverstone parish and her intimate knowledge of the area, Mrs Laverton has produced a clear account of how the settlement patterns have developed and changed over the last 2000 years. In addition, by including a survey of the archaeological and historical background for the region as a whole, the character and development of the peninsula can be judged against a wider background, which is invaluable for an area which has been both apparently isolated and self-contained while at the same time intimately linked with the world at large on the North Sea littoral.

The place-name and archaeological evidence has been treated with rigour and respect. Given the limitations involved in examining names from not just one but nine parishes and archaeological information collected by a variety of means, some areas are inevitably better illustrated than others. The end result is a clearly laid out survey of the place-name and archaeological evidence for the Shotley Peninsula which highlights numerous areas for future research.

The interplay between the two sources is tantalising, with the wealth of minor name evidence indicating where future research might be fruitful. Mrs Laverton clearly demonstrates how more archaeological fieldwork is vital for a further understanding of the peninsula. In particular, the amount of evidence for Scandinavian or Viking settlement amongst the minor names in some of the nine parishes is exciting as the extent and character of the Danish settlement in East Anglia is often debated but has rarely been systematically researched.

That this book brings so much place-name and archaeological evidence together in one place is a great credit to the author. The potential for future research is of great importance and I am sure that the book will inspire others to look in more detail at documents to further place-name studies, and at the landscape to reach fuller understanding of how the region has developed over the past 2000 years.

John Newman
Archaeological Service
Suffolk County Council
November 2000

Introduction

This book is about the early history of the Shotley Peninsula from the Late Iron Age to the Norman Conquest, explored through its place-names and the area's growing archaeological record which stretches back in time to periods beyond the reach of place-names. The events occurring during these thousand years had a decisive effect on the peninsula's landscape.

Some of the nine parishes that lie between the Orwell and Stour estuaries, so forming the peninsula, have excellent manorial and other early records from which place-names have been collected. For others, early documentary sources are scarce. Inevitably coverage has been uneven with no certainty that the earliest names have been traced. No doubt the picture will become clearer as progress is made with the Suffolk Place-Names Project. Names are generated by the interplay of people, places and contemporary history. The synthesis presented here shows that, despite its marginal location on the southern fringe of the county, the evolution of settlement in the area has been significantly affected by the many changes occurring in the wider world during the first millennium AD.

Nearly 50 years ago F.T. Wainwright identified the problems likely to beset those who attempt to apply archaeology and place-names to illuminate history: specialists in each field have their own different perspectives. This book has been written in the hope that a non-specialist's view, based on much research and advice tempered by frank criticism, can make a useful contribution to understanding the history of settlement in the Shotley Peninsula.

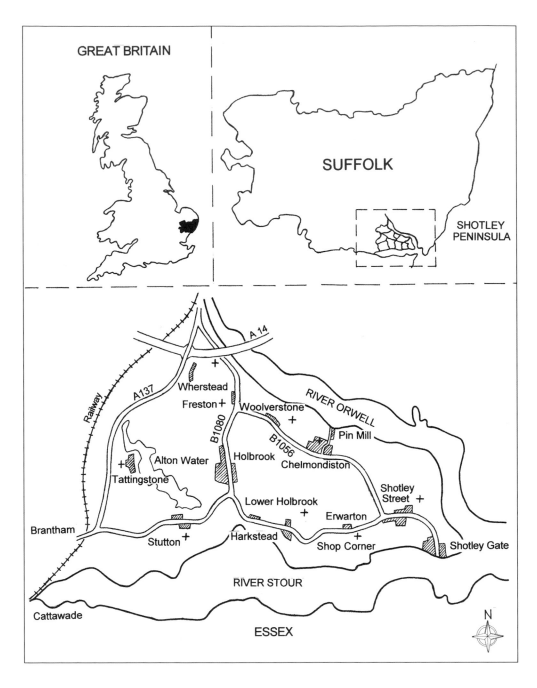

1 The Shotley Peninsula in south-east Suffolk: an area of scattered hamlets

1 The Shotley Peninsula

Suffolk's Shotley Peninsula lies in the furthermost south-eastern corner of the county, bounded by two tidal rivers, the Orwell and the Stour (**1**). It is generally perceived as remote and isolated. Seen only from the main roads that pass through it, the peninsula appears to be a random scatter of small villages, tiny hamlets and farmsteads surrounded by their fields — apparently a place of no great interest. But closer investigation reveals a network of narrow lanes, ancient trackways and footpaths that demonstrate the essential unity of an area which has had a long and varied history.

This well-defined, close-knit territory, surrounded by tidal waters, is occupied by nine parishes (**2**): Wherstead, Freston, Woolverstone and Chelmondiston bounded by the river Orwell; Erwarton, Harkstead, Holbrook and Stutton by the

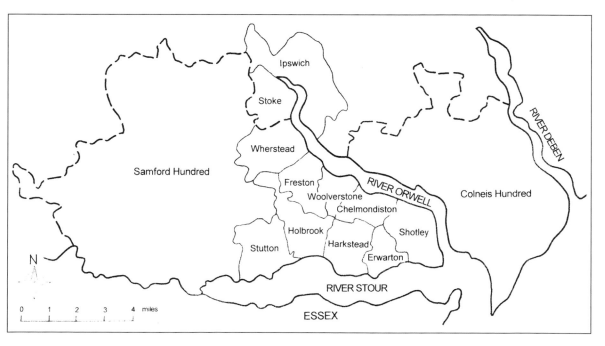

2 Nine parishes in the former Samford Hundred are bounded by the tidal rivers Orwell and Stour which flow into the North Sea; nineteenth-century parish boundaries. (Courtesy Suffolk County Council)

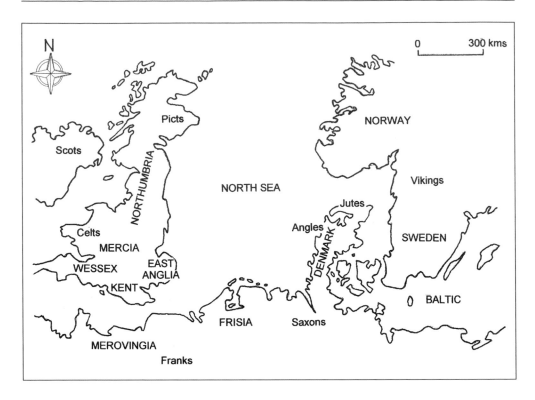

3   East Anglia and its North Sea neighbours. (Courtesy Peter Warner)

river Stour; and Shotley, at the blunt end of the peninsula, by both rivers where they converge to form the Orwell Haven and flow into the North Sea (**3**). These nine parishes provide an opportunity to explore the early history of an area unlike any other in Suffolk, where recent progress in archaeological fieldwork is providing new information about pre-Domesday settlement.

Environs

Two important factors have shaped the landscape of the Shotley Peninsula, one geographical, the other geological.

Though isolated from the main landmass of Suffolk by the watercourse that forms the northern boundary of Wherstead parish (Belstead Brook and the River Bourne) the peninsula has always had direct access by water to the North Sea and Northern Europe. Erosion and changes in the relative levels of land and water have altered the shorelines many times in the past — and are still doing so — but tidal creeks, hards, sandy bays and mud flats have provided ways into and out of the peninsula from prehistoric times. Many remained in use until superseded in the nineteenth century by road transport.[1] Present-day marinas and sailing clubs maintain links with Europe forged thousands of years ago. These links have had a fundamental influence on development in the peninsula.

Millions of years ago the last ice sheet of the Anglian Glaciation stopped short of the land surface that eventually became the Shotley and Felixstowe peninsulas. Their loamy surface soils — derived from loess, overlying sands and gravels — are uniquely different from those of the rest of Suffolk. Like Shotley Peninsula, Felixstowe Peninsula is bounded on two sides by tidal rivers — the Orwell and Deben — but it also extends into the North Sea. From the third century AD, when a Roman shore fort and harbour existed on this sea coast, Felixstowe Peninsula has had well-defined overland access to the hinterland. Modern Felixstowe and its internationally important container port are linked to the national road network by a trunk road.

It was not until 1972, when the Ipswich southern bypass was routed through Wherstead parish, that Shotley Peninsula finally gained direct access to Britain's modern road system. For hundreds of years there had been only two main overland routes out of the area — one over Bourne Bridge to Ipswich, the other over Cattawade Bridge into Essex. Before these bridges were built the only land routes would have been cross-country tracks or causeways over tidal water but from time immemorial waterways have given the peninsula's inhabitants unlimited access to places both within and beyond their home territory.

Geology and soils

The pattern of settlement and way of life in Shotley Peninsula have been shaped by geological changes taking place over many millions of years.

Chalk, the oldest rock, which underlies most of Suffolk, tilts downwards towards the eastern side of the county and lies too deep below the coastal areas to affect them. The lower slopes of the peninsula are London Clay, laid down as silty mud in a sea about 50 million years ago. Resting on the London Clay, deposits of sandy Red Crag, rich in fossil shells, occur throughout the peninsula. Where Red Crag and London Clay meet at the spring-line, streams emerge and occasionally there are minor landslips.

Overlying the Crag and forming the surface of most of the peninsula are the Kesgrave Sands and Gravels, rich in flint and quartz pebbles. They were deposited by the ancestral River Thames as it flowed north-eastwards through this part of Suffolk about 800,000 years ago.

During an intense cold phase about 400,000 years ago, a major ice-sheet advanced southwards into Suffolk as far as the western edge of the Shotley and Felixstowe peninsulas. When the ice melted, the clay and rock debris it carried left a layer of sticky intractable boulder clay covering almost the whole of Suffolk, except the two peninsulas and a narrow strip of coastal land to their north. Later ice-sheets reached no further than the north Norfolk coast.

The estuaries that now define the Shotley and Felixstowe peninsulas were once deep valleys that drained into the complex Rhine River System. When the last ice melted water levels rose and these valleys filled up with alluvium, becoming the Stour, Orwell and Deben estuaries. Post-glacial changes common to the two peninsulas left them with similar soils: quick-draining loamy soils derived from loess, with sands and gravels on the higher ground and heavier clay land near the rivers.

In Shotley Peninsula local variations in the composition of the surface and sub-soils are widespread. Field-names show that deposits of clay, crag, sands and gravels have been exploited in every parish over long periods. A Wherstead field called Lampets — loam pits — in the thirteenth century records the widespread practice of 'marling', in which loam (sandy clay), marl (calcareous clay), sand, or crag, were spread over arable fields to improve texture or correct acidity.

Most parishes had a Brick Field or Clamp Field where brick earth (a kind of clay) was used in brick making. This material was used to make bricks and tiles at a medieval tileyard beside the Orwell in Woolverstone where broken peg-tiles and misshapen bricks still litter the shore.

The beds of clayey limestone — septaria — which form the base of the peninsula's low coastal cliffs have not generated any field-names but this excellent building material can be seen in the walls and towers of many local churches. Apart from nodules of flint and mudstone, this is the only local building material. Fifteen Warren field-names listed in the Erwarton Tithe Apportionment define a large tract of sandy soil, once devoted to rabbit farming. Warren Lane still crosses this area.

Topography

The nine parishes of Shotley Peninsula occupy *c*.15,000 acres of land that rarely rises above 100ft, surrounded by *c*.1660 acres of tidal water and *c*.2800 acres of foreshore.[2] A flat central plateau forms a watershed below which spring-fed streams emerge, forming steep little valleys on the north side of the peninsula, and two longer ones further east. On the south side longer meandering water-courses flow into the Stour. The brook that gives Holbrook parish its name, the River Bourne that forms most of Wherstead's northern boundary and the Samford River that separates Stutton from Brantham, all rise outside the peninsula.

Though the peninsula lacks height overall, local variations in the contours result in a landscape in which level tracts are broken by unexpectedly steep slopes.

The whole is fringed by sandy bays and creeks, mudflats, and saltings washed by the tides. In some places there are low wooded cliffs. Old sea walls, recently raised and strengthened against rising water levels, surround marshland in Shotley parish and protect some low-lying farmland elsewhere.

Land-use

For thousands of years the main occupation of the peninsula's inhabitants has been farming. Although many fields have been enlarged in recent years to accommodate modern farm machinery, this is not wholly a 'prairie' area. The main arable crops are wheat, barley, sugar beet and potatoes. The brilliant yellow flowers of oil-seed rape and the blue haze of flax (linseed) in flower sometimes provide vivid contrast to the ubiquitous green and gold. Grassland is rare; silage is made from sweet corn. Recovered marshland and the few remaining meadows provide grazing for cattle. There are very few dairy herds and seldom many sheep. The heathlands that once occupied much of the central plateau and are still remembered in field-names have long been converted to arable cropping. Two parishes retain commons — at least in name. Chelmondiston's commons were taken into the Berners Estate in the nineteenth century but the sites still exist, cherished by the parish council. In Shotley parish the ancient Calton Common is named, incorrectly, Shotley Common on recent OS maps.

Woods and trees

Woodland is scarce in the peninsula. Holbrook Park, referred to as John de Holbroc's Park in the thirteenth century, is one of the most important historic woods in Suffolk. It may have been a deer park though there is no documentary proof. The enormous stools of coppiced sweet chestnut that exist in parts of the wood are among the largest recorded in Britain.[3] Three other woods close to Holbrook Park — Freston Wood, Cutlers Wood and Stalls Valley Wood — were also typical ancient woodland, but replanting was necessary after severe gale damage in 1987 drastically altered them. Dench Wood in Woolverstone, now derelict, was once extensive manorial wood pasture.

Elsewhere small areas of neglected coppice recall earlier times when managed woodland was an important asset. Most of the present-day woods were planted in the eighteenth century as game coverts or more recently for commercial production of softwood. New hardwood plantations are being established on the Green Estate in Harkstead.

Individual trees of enormous girth mark the bounds of early territories. Not all are on parish boundaries. An oak near Deer Park Lodge in Woolverstone has a girth of 37ft. A hideously gnarled field maple in the purlieus of the former Freston Manor Hall is reputed to be 1000 years old.

Church and community

The pattern of habitation in Shotley Peninsula is one of scattered hamlets, rows of houses lining roads and lanes, and isolated farmhouses and cottages. Housing estates built in the past half-century have given Chelmondiston, Holbrook and Stutton village centres but only the two former are grouped round their respective churches. The churches at Wherstead, Freston, Woolverstone, Shotley, Erwarton and Harkstead stand apart from the communities they now serve though there is documentary evidence indicating that manor halls existed near to all of them in the Middle Ages.

The reasons for this dispersed pattern, characteristic of much of rural Suffolk, lie in the past, partly in the years following the Norman Conquest but also in the preceding millennium.

2 Historical background

This brief and selective account of the course of English history from the Late Iron Age to 1066 is focused specifically on eastern England, East Anglia and the area that became the county of Suffolk, with the aim of emphasising events and trends which may have affected Shotley Peninsula. It reflects current opinion which may well change as archaeological research continues to add new information about the period.

In the first century BC tribal kingdoms with regional centres (oppida) emerged. The area which became south Suffolk, north-east Essex and Hertfordshire was occupied by the Trinovantes and the Catuvellauni; the Iceni's territory lay further north. Immigrant Belgic tribesmen from Gaul strongly influenced the culture of southern Britain, though areas further north, including the Iceni territory, were largely outside the influence of 'Belgicisation'.[1] Julius Caesar sent expeditions into Britain in 55 and 54 BC, exacted promises of tribute and concluded some treaties with local tribal kings. The south and east of Britain grew increasingly rich through exchange and trade with Gaul and the Roman Empire. In the early years of the first century AD Cunobelin, king of the Catuvellauni, acquired Trinovantian territory and gained immense power and wealth through his command of key trade routes to the Continent. These included links via the Colne and Stour estuaries, used most probably by his own ships (**4**).[2]

Cunobelin died *c*.AD 40. In 43 Roman legions of the Emperor Claudius invaded, destroyed the Iron Age oppidum at Camulodunum, and built a legionary fortress there from which Colchester developed as the first Roman town in Britain.

The devastating tribal revolt led by Boudicca in 61 was suppressed. Conquest of England was followed by the extension of Roman rule into Wales and southern Scotland: Britain became Britannia, a province of the Roman Empire. Within 100 years of the Claudian invasion southern Britain was heavily Romanised, with a road network, towns, a money economy, markets and efficient systems of administration and taxation. The rural population grew prosperous as agricultural and industrial production expanded to meet the demands of urban and export markets and the Roman army. Evidence for this prosperity has been found on

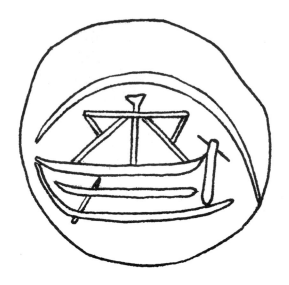

4 *A rare coin of Cunobelin minted in Sheepen (Camulodunum) illustrates a trading ship of the period — not to scale. (Courtesy Oxford Institute of Archaeology)*

many of the small farm sites which were integrated with the cash economy and were receiving goods such as pots from distant sources.

Second-century unrest on Britain's northern frontier was countered, but in Europe barbarian pressure increased and by the mid-third century piracy was a serious threat. A chain of coastal forts capable of safe-guarding sea routes to and from the Continent was built in the late third century between Brancaster on the north Norfolk coast and Portchester in Hampshire. The fort at Walton (Felixstowe) (**5**) — 'Walton Castle' — and another believed to have existed at Walton (Essex), were well sited to guard Suffolk's Deben, Orwell and Stour estuaries and the Blackwater and Colne estuaries in north Essex. Both forts have been swallowed by the sea. Neither appears in the Notitia Dignitatum. The Felixstowe fort is well attested by archaeological and documentary evidence.[3] There is no archaeological evidence for the Essex fort, but Hart suggests that the District called The Naze — Edulvesnaesa 'Eadwulf's Promontary' — which includes Walton, must have been a haven if not an active sea port as late as 1052.[4] Fourth-century Britain, initially prosperous, was invaded by Picts and Scots and harassed by barbarian war bands until order was restored by Theodosius the Elder in AD 367, but Rome's western empire was disintegrating under internal tensions and threats to the central provinces from the east.

For a time the British economy remained buoyant — some new villas were built (though not in East Anglia); the ceramic industry expanded in the absence of imports from northern Europe — but in the second half of the fourth century activity in East Anglia was declining and some sites had apparently been abandoned or had ceased to receive the coinage then in circulation. Early in the fifth century the Roman army was withdrawn. The import of new bullion into Britain ended and, by *c*.420, the use of coinage had ceased.

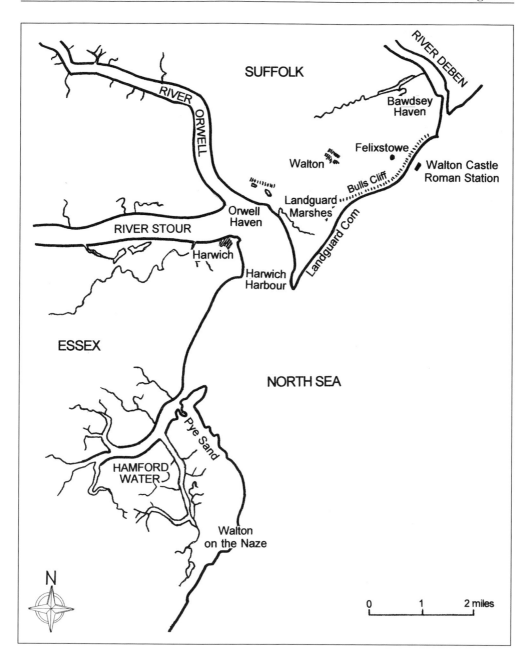

5 *The ruins of the cliff-top site of the Roman fort at Walton (Felixstowe) fell into the sea in the eighteenth century; any remaining stonework is now beyond the low tide mark. Cliff erosion also claimed the fort believed to have occupied a cliff-top site at Walton, Essex, though stone recovered from the sea in the vicinity has not been authenticated as Roman material. (Redrawn from VCH Suffolk)*

By then Britain had broken from Roman rule. The subsequent fate of the British population remains a matter for conjecture. Farming apparently continued, with output sufficient to sustain reduced demand by the now substantially rural population. It is likely that some areas remained under local Romano-British control well into the fifth century, possibly with some protection by Anglo-Saxon mercenary settlers.

By the mid-fifth century Britain's population had become a complex ethnic mixture. Native Britons, barbarians already present as Romano-Germanic mercenaries, and disbanded units of the Roman army (of various ethnic origins) were joined by Germanic and Scandinavian people from the Continent. How these incomers became dominant is still an open question. Whether they came as immigrants or as intending conquerors is still unclear, but by the end of the fifth century most of Britain was under Anglo-Saxon control.

Initial settlements expanded in East Anglia, Kent and Sussex. In East Anglia the Wuffinga dynasty reigned until King Edmund was murdered by the Danes in 869. King Raedwald, whose power and influence spread beyond East Anglia, died in *c.*624. Though he accepted Christian baptism, he was buried in pagan splendour at Sutton Hoo on the east bank of the river Deben. The rich variety of objects buried with him shows how far-reaching the trade and exchange routes were at that time. Bruce-Mitford suggested that the finds from Mound 1 Ship Burial — Raedwald's grave — had come from Scandinavia, France, Italy and the Eastern Mediterranean.[5] Later, analysis and reconstruction of the grave's treasures at the British Museum led to the idea that the sword, shield and helmet were made by Swedish craftsmen working at the East Anglian court, perhaps using dies made in Scandinavia.[6] The silver objects were probably made in east Mediterranean workshops, reaching north-west Europe by the riverine trade routes, and ending in East Anglia via Merovingian Gaul as a diplomatic gift. Martin Carver's account of Sutton Hoo includes a review of settlement and agriculture at the site from *c.*3000 BC to AD 600 and discusses its role as a royal burial ground.[7]

In Britain, both Britons and Romans worshipped many gods.[8] The Christian faith, initially introduced into Britain by Roman forces and administrators and by traders, was never entirely lost despite persecution in the third century. Following Constantine's conversion Christianity gained adherents throughout Britain, but the majority of inhabitants probably remained pagan. Christian beliefs and practices retained a tenuous hold until Augustine arrived in Kent in AD 597 charged by the Pope with the task of converting Britain's pagan population. Ascendancy of the Roman Church was achieved by the establishment of bishoprics, the foundation of monasteries that provided for personal devotion, and minster churches which acted as centres from which pastoral care was extended over large areas. Eventually parish churches were built to serve local communities; until then minster priests were permitted to say Mass 'in the field' at sites marked by a standing cross.

The first English see was founded in East Anglia in AD 630 by Sigeberht, Raedwald's Christian son. The first bishop — Felix, an Irish-born Burgundian monk — established his see at a place referred to as Domnoc in ASC (F) (636) and as Domnoc/Dommoc by Bede.[9] These names have been interpreted as Dunwich but it is more likely that Felix built his church within the walls of the Roman fort at Walton (Felixstowe).

There is archaeological evidence of an Early Saxon settlement and a pagan cemetery in the vicinity of the Roman fort site.[10] Early churches built within the walls of Roman forts are known elsewhere, for example at Othona (Bradwell) on the Essex coast. Place-name evidence favours the Felixstowe site. Ekwall suggested that the first element in these names may have been Celtic *dubno* 'dark deep' which, combined with OE *wic* 'town or port', would mean Dunwich, but a gloss in *Cotton's Chronicles* (1298) translates as 'Domnoc which is called Filchestowe by the sea in East Suffolk'. This, cited by Rigold with other evidence, identifies Domnoc with Felixstowe (Walton).[11] In a recent analysis of the place-name evidence Coates concludes that Felix' see was indeed at Felixstowe (Walton). Dunwich was Dunewic (DB) in which the first element OE *dun* may mean simply 'dune, sandhill'. Domnoc/Dommoc derived from Late Latin *dominicum*, the source of Irish *domhnach* 'church', with OE *stowe*, 'site of periodic assembly typically associated with a saint', explains Felixstowe as 'Felix's place of periodic assembly': the site of Felix' see.[12]

Despite the power of the Roman church, long-established pagan practices remained evident 100 years after Augustine's arrival in 597. Theodore, archbishop of Canterbury, appointed penances for those who continued in the ancient ways but in remote country places pagan sites continued to be venerated for many more years.[13] The growing influence of the Church led indirectly to basic changes in land tenure. Land belonging originally to large royal estates was granted to support new religious foundations as well as to members of royal households. From the eighth century, charters recorded widespread land transactions and later, land sold outright was further divided through inheritance, thus producing the manorial economy recorded in the Domesday Survey. While fragmentation of royal estates continued, sporadic warfare among the earlier kingdoms led to the expansion of the more powerful until, for a brief period in the late eighth century, the Mercian king Offa ruled all Britain south of the Humber.

Ipswich (Gipeswic), originally established as a trading centre on the north bank of the Orwell at the head of the estuary, became an important international port in the Middle Saxon period.[14]

In 865, the eastern half of the country was invaded and rapidly overrun by Danish armies whose men remained as settlers in the North and Midlands.

Elsewhere, the Danish forces met stubborn resistance from the Wessex dynasty. In 878 King Alfred fought and held the army of the Danish king Guthrum at Edington in Wiltshire. Under the agreement that followed, Alfred accepted the Danish occupation of eastern England as a *fait accompli* and Guthrum agreed to withdraw his army to East Anglia which he was to rule as king. Accordingly, in 880 Guthrum led his men there and took possession of the land.[15] What followed is usually described as 'sharing out the land'. This explains the pattern of widespread Danish settlements in the north, but in East Anglia 'dividing' seems the more appropriate translation, for as place-name evidence suggests, the number of Danish settlers seems to have been small.[16] The territory ruled by Guthrum and his successors, from 880 until it was reconquered by the Wessex king Edward the Elder in 921, became known as the Eastern Danelaw, its western borders guarded by a series of dykes and large areas of swampy fenland. The full extent of the Danelaw territory is detailed in the Ordnance Survey's Map of Britain before the Norman Conquest.[17] The evolution of the Eastern Danelaw is explored in detail by Cyril Hart.[18]

In the 990s a new series of short, sharp, pirate — Viking — raids began. In 991 a much larger force ravaged Ipswich and then encamped in Essex on Northey Island east of Maldon in the Blackwater Estuary. There, Brihtnoth, earldorman of Essex, died in a vain attempt to defeat the Viking host. The battle and the heroic poem that celebrates the event, and their place in the history of the late tenth and early eleventh centuries, are still the subject of critical comment.[19]

Money paid to Viking raiders to buy them off encouraged further widespread attacks. In 1010 Ipswich was sacked again. When, in 1013, king Swein of Denmark invaded, apparently intent on conquest, he was not opposed by Danish England. Though his attack on London failed, the Anglo-Saxon Chronicle records that the whole nation regarded him as king in all respects (ASC E). The English king Aethelred fled to Normandy, only returning after Swein died in 1014. In 1016, after Aethelred's death, his son Edmund was involved in several encounters with Cnut, Swein's son, finally losing the battle fought in October at Assandun, an unidentified place in Essex.[20] Hart summarises the arguments for the alternative sites, Ashington and Ashdon, in chapter 19 *The Danelaw* pp533-51. Edmund died in November 1016 and Cnut was accepted as king of England. Since he was also king of Denmark and Norway from 1019, Cnut appointed four earls to act for him when he was absent from England: two English, two Danish. In effect, an Anglo-Scandinavian aristocracy then governed England; gradually Danish separatedness faded and the Christian Cnut ruled as lord of both Danes and non-Danes.

From 1042, after the death of Cnut and the brief reigns of his two sons, the Wessex kings became de facto rulers of England, restoring English law and applying their efficient systems of government and taxation where Danish custom had been the rule. Edward the Confessor died in 1066. Harold Godwineson, Earl of Wessex, then became king of England. His defeat by William of Normandy at Hastings nine months later ended 600 years of Saxon rule.

William was crowned king of England in December 1066. He made fundamental changes to the old-established system of land tenure, replacing Saxon landholders with Normans who 'held of the king' for military service. The Domesday Survey of Norfolk, Suffolk and Essex (Domesday Book volume ii, or Little Domesday Book) is an unabridged compilation of the statistical data collected by King William's commissioners charged with the task of finding out what land he had and who held it.[21]

DB ii records in minute detail the names of each estate and small holding, its agricultural assets, manpower, value and taxable acreage, as it was in the time of Edward the Confessor ('then') and again in 1086 ('now'). Information about the interim period is also included in some instances. The Survey is arranged under the names of the new Norman holders.

The Norman Conquest ended the centuries-long progress from the small nameless farmsteads of the Late Iron Age, through the development of the Romano-British, Saxon and Scandinavian settlements to the townships, vills and free mens' holdings described in the Domesday Survey. How this transformation came about is largely beyond the reach of historical research. The contributions that archaeology and place-name studies may be able to make in tracing developments in Shotley Peninsula are explored in the following chapters.

3 Archaeology

Techniques

Archaeology was once famously defined as 'digging up the past'. This eye-catching phrase entirely fails to convey the modern meaning of the subject, which has evolved from the early study of antiquities into a highly specialised discipline that involves much more than digging.

Though excavation — 'digging' in a systematic and meticulously recorded way — remains the basic activity, opportunities to excavate have been greatly circumscribed by legislation designed to preserve 'heritage sites' for future generations and, not least, by cost. The official guidance notes allow for preservation in situ of sites of national interest. Investigation of other sites by recorded excavation is affected by development proposals. Archaeology is therefore a material consideration in planning matters, with the result that fieldwork is carried out in areas of high development pressure. In Shotley Peninsula, where local plans allow for little more than village infill and minor small-scale development work, places where no development is contemplated have to be investigated by techniques other than excavation. PPG 16 — Planning Policy Guidance — recognising the importance of archaeology, sets out official guidelines intended to ensure that development is managed so as to ensure that archaeological remains survive in good condition or, where this is not feasible, they are 'preserved by record'. Nationally important sites receive special protection as 'scheduled monuments'.[1]

Geophysical methods for recording below-ground irregularities, invaluable for mapping known sites, are expensive. For surveying large areas of farmland there is a simple alternative: systematic field-walking allied with the responsible use of metal detectors. Success depends on three essentials: the landowners' interest and consent; accurate site records; and close liaison with the archaeologists who analyse, interpret and record the results. Surface finds plus metalwork recovered from the plough-soil of arable fields are providing new insights into the early history of East Anglia.[2]

These artefacts can indicate much more than the presence of the people who used them. For instance, chemical analysis of pottery fragments can show what the original vessel contained: traces of sodium chloride would indicate local production or transport of salt or salted fish; traces of milk fat would suggest the possibility of dairying in the vicinity. The composition of coins or metalwork, determined by chemical or physical methods, can indicate sources of raw materials and hence suggest trade links. Differences in the composition of coins minted at different periods mirror the changing economic circumstances in which they were produced. Sceattas (coinage in circulation *c*.AD 690-750) found in association with Ipswich-ware are important indicators of local trading and will eventually enable the production of Ipswich-ware to be dated with greater certainty.[3]

Cropmarks revealed by aerial photography may provide pointers to potentially interesting sites. In drought conditions uneven crop growth caused by the presence of old foundations, ditches, boundaries and trackways below the ground surface can cause variations in crop colour or differences in crop height clearly visible when photographed obliquely from the air. Since the 1970s several years of summer drought in Shotley Peninsula have produced ideal conditions for this type of survey. High altitude photographs taken vertically, generally for other purposes, can also locate underwater and inter-tidal structures.

The collections of aerial photographs held in the Suffolk County Sites and Monuments Records and in the library of the National Monuments Records Centre at Swindon now cover the entire Shotley Peninsula which is an area particularly prone to develop features readily recorded on air photographs. Unfortunately, interpretation is difficult for there is no certain way to differentiate between marks caused by features from different periods but the patterns produced by repeated surveys of comparatively large areas are becoming increasingly useful in settlement studies when looked at in conjunction with other evidence.

Field-walking on crop-marked sites can be productive but soils prone to develop them are exactly those with a long history of arable cultivation. Though the chances that fragile pottery will escape destruction by the plough grow slimmer as time goes by, each cultivation brings new material to the surface, so repeated 'walks' are necessary. Experience in the peninsula has shown that areas where metal detector users have already reported significant finds make the best targets for field-walkers.

Palaeoarchaeology — the analysis of soil core samples taken from farmland, marshland and inter-tidal sites — combined with carbon dating, is a valuable non-destructive method for tracing agrarian history over long periods of time. It has already produced valuable insights in East Anglia.[4]

The archaeology of Shotley Peninsula

Although Shotley Peninsula seldom offers opportunities for excavation, in recent years limited excavation has been possible in Wherstead, prior to gravel extraction, and trenches for sewerage and for new water pipelines have been investigated in several places. However, almost all the archaeological data discussed in detail in later chapters refer to finds made during the past 20 years, on and within the plough-soil where landowners have granted access to their fields. Most of the work has been concentrated on parishes bordering the Orwell; areas bounded by the Stour have received very little attention so far. The distribution of all finds at present on record reflects this bias rather than any fundamental differences between the two areas. As would be expected due to its friability, surface finds of hand-made Iron Age pottery are rare but some sherds of wheel-turned Late Iron Age Belgic-ware are on record. Iron Age coinage, mainly Trinovantian, has been recovered from several sites.

Material from the Roman period has been found in every parish but recovery of Saxon material is patchy. Neither pagan cemeteries nor individual burials are known and no Early Saxon pottery from the period AD 450-650 has been found. Field-walkers' failure to find Early Saxon pottery is hardly surprising, for this fabric has a 'life expectancy' of little more than 25 years in the ploughsoil (Colin Pendleton pers. comm.). Tangible indication of a Saxon presence from the seventh century onwards is attested by finds of Ipswich-ware (AD c.650-850) and Thetford-type ware (AD c.850-1150), a few silver sceattas (early to mid-eighth-century coinage) and a variety of Mid- and Late Saxon metalwork and related items. Carved stone dated to the tenth or eleventh century is visible in the outer walls of Stutton church (**6**).

No material of unequivocally Scandinavian (Viking) origin has been detected in the areas investigated. So far all finds of this period have been Anglo-Scandinavian objects dated to the tenth or eleventh century: a few metalwork items are decorated in styles that suggest Scandinavian influence.

A coherent account of settlement development in the peninsula is not yet possible — the finds are too few and much of the territory remains unexplored. However, place-names provide an additional, independent approach. The following chapter outlines their scope and limitations.

4 Place-names

Names and language; interpretation; value and limitations

The present-day names of hamlets, villages and towns, so familiar that they seldom arouse curiosity about their origins, are the end results of a long series of changes. In their earliest recorded forms most would be unrecognisable, for current names are the result of many changes in language, speech and spelling occurring over many hundreds of years. The earliest forms of place-names reflect the circumstances in which they were coined and so provide archaeologists and historians with information about early settlements and their environments. The languages from which modern English place-names have evolved include Celtic, Latin, Old English and Old Norse and Norman French. Celtic, the British language which formed the basis of Cornish and Welsh, was spoken all over England when the Roman armies invaded. Though Latin was the language of officialdom in Britain during Roman rule, few words of Latin origin have survived in settlement names. Celtic remained in general use in Britain until it was displaced by Old English introduced by the Germanic migrants who came to England in the fifth century. In turn Old English was modified in areas occupied by Danish settlers in the ninth century and also influenced by Norman French after the Conquest. Traces of all these different languages remain embedded in modern English and can be recognised in place-names dating from the earliest written records.

Since it was founded in 1923, specifically to survey the country's place-names, the English Place-Name Society has collected and analysed the names found in almost all the English counties and published the results in more than 70 volumes. The first volumes dealing with Norfolk appeared recently; preliminary work on Suffolk names began in 1998.

Interpreting these names — place-name etymology — is a strict linguistic discipline with its own well-established rules. Long experience has shown that the only way to arrive at a reliable explanation of a name is to collect as many versions as possible from written sources, including especially the earliest spellings. From these it is possible to deduce the form the word would have had in Old English or one of the other earlier languages. When this word is broken down into its basic elements it is usually possible to work out how the word was derived and so to determine its original meaning.

In settlement studies two interdependent factors are involved: the elements from which a place-name has been derived, which can provide a surprisingly accurate description of a site, and the local topography which can be a deciding factor when more than one meaning is possible. Field-walking is probably the best way to 'see' a site within the local landscape; walking local footpaths provides a wider view. Understanding the role of place-name elements is less simple.

A.H. Smith's *English Place-Name Elements*, published by the EPNS in 1956, includes a 20-page introduction in which he defines the term 'element'. He explains how grammatical usage and dialect variants affect the form an element can take and shows how a change in the character of a settlement can lead to change in the meaning of the word used to describe it.

For instance, the Old English topographical word *burna* meaning, originally, 'a stream', later became Bourn, the name of a settlement that grew up beside the water. The habitative element *-tūn*, originally denoting 'enclosure', acquired new meanings as the settlement expanded, so place-names ending in *-tūn* came to mean 'farmstead', 'village', 'estate', and eventually 'town'.

Place-names ending in *-tūn or -hām* denote places where people lived, the type of settlement being described by a variety of prefixes, for instance Old English *-dūn*, with *-tūn* interpreted as 'hill farm'. The genitive case, implying the idea of personal possession, occurs in names that describe land ownership, for instance Woolverstone was 'the estate of a man called Wulfhere'.

Specific details of individual interpretations are to be found in the appropriate reference books included in the bibliography (p142). Eilert Ekwall's *Oxford Dictionary of English Place-Names* first published in 1936 includes analyses of many ancient settlement names. A.H. Smith's *English Place-Name Elements* (two volumes 1987) contains an enormous amount of information about the elements from which place-names are constructed. Though these works are now somewhat out of date, for non-specialists searching for place-name meanings they will remain indispensable until the *Vocabulary of English Place-Names* being published by the Centre for English Names Studies, Nottingham, is completed. Two volumes are in print: *Á-Box* published in 1997 and *Brace-Caester* in 2000. A.D. Mills' *Oxford Dictionary of English Place-Names*, second edition 1998, includes some useful introductory sections on language, types of place-names and their wider significance. The late John Field's *History of English Field-Names* is also a valuable source of reference, for the names of fields, even relatively recent ones, can throw light on settlement history.

As in any type of research, theories are revised whenever new information is acquired. Interpretations of place-names are therefore liable to change. New concepts introduced by J.McN. Dodgson in 1966[1] and by Barrie Cox in 1974-5[2] superseded earlier views and stimulated continuing interest in place-name chronology and its role in settlement studies. More recently Margaret Gelling's detailed analyses of Britain's place-names in their historical and geographical contexts have demonstrated the fundamental importance of local topography in interpreting individual names.[3-5] Clearly the Anglo-Saxons had a huge topographical vocabulary that they employed very successfully in naming the places in which they lived.

Not all agree about the value of place-names as indicators of settlement sites. Certainly it would be unreasonable to imagine that a name coined many hundreds of years ago could be traced and used to mark an early settlement on a modern map, without much additional information. Settlements tended to shift and some undoubtedly changed their names to fit new locations. Changes in the meaning of a name's basic elements with time must therefore be allowed for: unless a site yields dateable artefacts its name can be interpreted only in broad terms.

The value of place-names in settlement studies lies in their ubiquity and abundance and in the remarkable accuracy with which they describe local terrain. It is these characteristics that allow them to reinforce the findings of archaeology especially where the local topography and its past history are well understood.

This book combines recent archaeological research and current ideas about local place-names to provide a limited and speculative account of the history of Shotley Peninsula through the first millennium AD.

5 Settlement evolution

In the following pages the names of places and people are used to augment the tangible evidence of pre-Conquest settlement in Shotley Peninsula currently being accumulated by archaeological methods. For ease of reference sites are reviewed in terms of parishes as defined by their modern (pre-1974) boundaries; their earliest boundaries were not fixed until the twelfth century.

Sources — a critical evaluation

Names have been taken from the author's collection. The derivations and meanings suggested in the text are based on the publications of the English Place-Names Society and other sources discussed in the previous chapter.

The archaeological data has been extracted from the Suffolk Sites and Monuments Records (SMR) (**6**). Chapter 14 lists the locations of all the Shotley Peninsula sites dating from the Late Iron Age (100 BC-AD 43) to 1066, recorded to December 1998; brief details are included of individual finds for each period: Late Iron Age, Roman (Romano-British) and Saxon (including Anglo-Scandinavian). Maps indicating findspots are included in the text. The present-day shorelines shown on these maps are the result of erosion, silting and reclamation occurring over many hundreds of years, so due caution is needed in relating these to individual archaeological sites.

Place-names recorded before the Norman Conquest are rare throughout East Anglia. Few charters recording land transactions made before the Viking incursion escaped destruction, and early narrative sources lack specific reference to the area. Bede's reference to Rendlesham as the king's country-seat in the province of the East Angles is an exception.[1] Only two pre-1086 documents relating specifically to Shotley Peninsula are on record: the Stoke Charter and the Will of Aelflaed, widow of earldorman Bryhtnoth (1000-2). The Stoke Charter (CS 1269:8, AD 970) records King Edgar's gift of Stoke by Ipswich to the Abbey of Ely. It includes the name of a ford in Wherstead, translated by Cyril Hart as 'thief's ford'.[2] Aelfflaed's will mentions her estate in Freston but gives no details.[3]

Apart from these, the earliest recorded place-names of the Shotley Peninsula appear in volume ii of the Domesday Book.[4] These 1066 Domesday place-names represent the final phase of Saxon (and Danish) settlement. Many have persisted

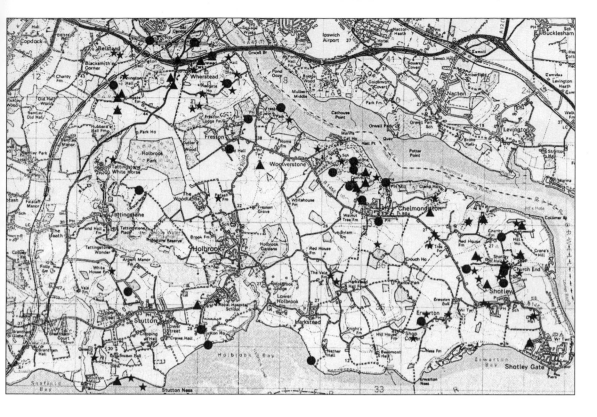

6   *Map: all first millennium archaeological sites on record in 1998. The distribution of findspots shows activity concentrated within reach of the peninsula's waterways. Recorded sites are rare in the south, which has not yet been explored systematically. (Map Suffolk SMR) Key: Late Iron Age ▲; Roman period ★; Saxon period ●*

in modified forms in the names of present-day estates and farms: seven became parish names.

Most of the names discussed here were recorded no earlier than the thirteenth century and collections of spellings are rarely possible. Conclusions drawn from such data are unavoidably speculative. Even so, some local names appear to carry memories of long-ago communities. A significant number corroborate archaeological findings and a few point to the existence of settlements previously unsuspected.

Settlement — an overview

The archaeological record of Shotley Peninsula indicates three phases of settlement in the thousand years between the end of the Iron Age and the advent of the Normans: Celtic, Saxon and Anglo-Scandinavian. For nearly half of this time, most of it in the Roman era, British (Celtic) people occupied sites overlooking the estuaries of the Orwell and Stour. At present there is not enough evidence to show how these farmsteads — some perhaps clustered as hamlets — were related to one another and to later, post-Roman patterns of habitation. From evidence across East Anglia as a whole it is clear that many of these sites had their origins in the Bronze and Iron Ages: the basis for the structure of the landscape in the earliest years of the first millennium AD was laid down in the preceding thousand years. During the Roman era and the years immediately before, the peninsula's farmers, working light, well-watered land and aided by the development of new crop varieties and improved tools, were producing a surplus which they traded profitably. Though crops and livestock were the primary products, output included pottery, wool, leather, bone and iron tools, fish and salt. After the withdrawal of the Roman army early in the fifth century some rural settlements were abandoned but it seems possible that on some sites the Romano-British way of life may have continued largely undisturbed until the emergence of the East Anglian Kingdom in the sixth century. With one possible exception — Climston in Harkstead — no Shotley Peninsula place-names containing Celtic elements have been traced in the course of this research. From *c*.600 the archaeological record and local place- and field-names reflect the influence of migrants from Europe. Though not all were from Saxony, the name Saxon is used to define the three archaeological periods — Early, Mid- and Late Saxon respectively — that provide a convenient framework in which to examine settlement evolution between *c*.450 and 1066.

The incomers and their descendants increased in numbers and added new settlements to the landscape. This trend was not greatly affected by the arrival of the Danish warrior king Guthrum who came with his army to settle in East Anglia in 880. One new settlement — Thorp — was founded in the peninsula, some Old English place-names acquired Scandinavian forms, and some surnames, personal- and field-names of the period show Danish influence. It seems that the Vikings and Danes who settled in the Shotley Peninsula were assimilated peacefully into local society. Most of them occupied land that eventually formed part of the parishes of Shotley, Erwarton and Harkstead. By that time the trend toward estates bearing the holders' names was well established all over the peninsula.

At the Conquest much of the land in the Shotley Peninsula was in royal hands. Taxation and valuation figures recorded in the Suffolk volume of the Domesday Survey indicate how profitable the lands in the peninsula had become during the Danelaw years and the final reversion to Saxon control.

6 The Celtic years: Late Iron Age and Romano-British sites

The earliest Iron Age farms were small, scattered and not enclosed. During the last millennium BC an increasing population competing for the limited amount of land available for cultivation led, in some areas, to demarcation of home territories by enclosure within banks and ditches or palisades.[1] Rural settlements in Roman Britain are discussed by Hingley.[2] Evidence from field-walking, aerial photography and place-names indicates that in the Late Iron Age and Romano-British periods there were numerous settlements all round the Shotley Peninsula

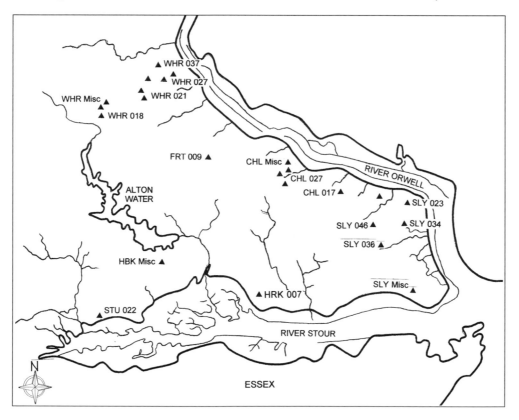

7   Late Iron Age sites cluster near to water sources. (SMR map redrawn)

mostly at or above the 50ft contour. Whether any of the recorded sites and others recognised only from aerial photographs were originally enclosed is impossible to judge, for arable cultivation with modern farm machinery has removed all visible earthwork evidence of ancient enclosure.

Defended sites

Eastern England lacks massive hillforts but defensible sites characteristic of the Iron Age do exist, positioned to ensure a difficult approach over water or through open country.[3] Three possible defended sites in the Shotley Peninsula indicated by place-names or topographical evidence lie close to the Orwell or the Stour on hilltops. Elbury, named in Elbury Down (1683), has been identified with a site in Woolverstone at the end of a hollow lane called Dontonstrete in 1491 (Mannings Lane now). The hilltop is a gravel platform guarded by a deeply cut watercourse on the east, a steep slope to the west and a northerly face that descends steeply in two stages — separated by a shallow ditch — to the Orwell Shore. The site (TM 1849 3914) is concealed now in woodland (**41**, p71). Archaeological investigation has not yet been permitted. The meaning of the name Elbury is 'old fortified place', OE *burh*, often denoting an ancient pre-English earthwork or encampment.[4] Documentary evidence places a British farmstead (Walton) in the vicinity.[5]

In Shotley parish a defended site may have occupied the high land at the tip of the peninsula where Bristol Hill rises abruptly from the Stour shore (TM 2485 3360). Strategically, this would have been an excellent defensive site but confirmation is difficult. Derelict woodland on the steep side overlooking the estuary effectively conceals any sign of ditches and the hilltop is now occupied by a group of immobile caravans.

A third possible defended site may have occupied land overlooking the Orwell in Freston Park (TM 1780 3691). The former manor hall (now three dwellings) stands on a prominent hilltop from which the land slopes down to the water in a series of terraces. This situation would have allowed ample warning of attack from the river. However, there is no supporting archaeological or place-name evidence.

Unrecorded embanked sites

Names implying the former existence of banks, ditches or palisades occur in the documentary records of Chelmondiston, Wherstead, Shotley and Harkstead.

Affoswalle[6] — 'at the ditched embankment' from OE *foss* 'a ditch' with OE (Angl) 'a rampart for defence' — was a sixteenth-century tenement near

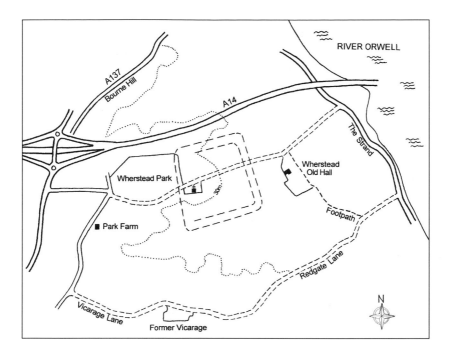

8 *A large rectangular embanked enclosure between Wherstead church and the Old Hall was revealed by aerial photography. Ploughing has levelled the area; no dating evidence has yet been found. (Drawn from SMR photograph)*

Chelmondiston church.[7] The description fits the topography of a site north of present-day Chelmondiston Church Farmhouse where the northern field boundary is marked by an impressively large bank. Supporting evidence is provided by the Tithe Map field-name Walton — 'walled farm' or 'native British settlement' — referring to land adjacent to the banked field.

Several Wherstead deeds of the late thirteenth century include 'wall' names: Sparnis Walton; Knawebonwall Meadow; Knoubones Wall (a boundary) and the surname John atte Wall. The name Sparrwalton was still used there in the seventeenth century.[8] Sparnis may have been a personal-name (so far not identified) but derivation from OE *spearr*, *spaer*, 'a spar', could point to a settlement enclosed within a palisade.[9] An aerial photograph (WHR 039) (**8**) shows clearly the outline of a large rectangular embanked enclosure on land sloping eastwards from the church to Wherstead Old Hall. Excavation of a trench close to the northern edge of the site yielded a scatter of Neolithic and Bronze Age flints and nothing of note from later periods; field-walking may provide additional data.

In a 1380 rental of Kirkton manor, translated by S.H.A. Hervey, Walter de Peryes was named as a former tenant of 'Belished'. This entry had been crossed out, and the tenement's name altered to Swenyehed, held by the Rector of Kerketon. Swineshead is named on the Shotley Tithe Map (1839) and listed as glebe land in 1911.[10] If the name given as 'Belished' was a misreading for Belisted or Belsted, it would have indicated a cremation site: bel-stede, *baelstede*, OE 'the place of a funeral pyre', the derivation suggested for the nearby Suffolk parish Belstead and also for Belstead in Essex.[11] Unfortunately it is impossible to confirm this reading as the original rental has been lost.

In Harkstead parish aerial photographs show two enclosures (**9** & **10**). One is an irregular D-shaped enclosure with internal trackways of a type rare in East Anglia. The site, recorded as 'undated ?Iron Age', lies at 50ft on a natural plateau facing south over the Stour in an extensive area of field systems and trackways. It is a Scheduled Ancient Monument (HRK 007; SAM 182 27881).

Harkstead glebe terriers record that in the sixteenth and seventeenth centuries a piece of glebeland called Martle Bourn(e) was bounded 'on the south by a creek of the sea flowing from Harwich to Manningtree' (ie the Stour estuary). This piece of glebeland became farmland called Myrtle Bones in 1839 (Tithe Map) and Mortal Bones now. Its southern boundary is in marshy land beside the estuary. Martle may be derived from OE (*ge*)*maere* 'a boundary' with OE *burna* 'a stream'.[12] This description fits a Stourside area due south of the D-shaped site, where an ancient creek since lost by erosion would have provided access to the sea. SMR's master site map indicates a second creek, now mostly silted, which may also have been associated with this settlement site.

9 A 1990 aerial photograph of a Harkstead field near the Stour revealed cropmarks of a D-shaped embanked enclosure. Ten years' ploughing had destroyed the banks. (Photograph I. MacMaster)

10 A second embanked site and associated field system in north-west Harkstead was seen in a 1990 aerial photograph. It has not yet been investigated. (Photograph I. MacMaster)

Other Late Iron Age and Romano-British settlement sites

Wherstead parish has proved particularly rich in Late Iron Age and Roman period sites. Limited excavation at the top of Bourne Hill (WHR 037) in 1989/90 provided evidence of numerous ditches containing Late Iron Age and first-century Roman material: sherds of handmade and local 'Belgic' wheel-thrown pottery, Roman grey-ware, some Gaulish samian-ware and fragments of a Dressel 2-4 wine amphora. Two copper-alloy coins are recorded as Trinovantian types: one is stylistically pre-Cunobelin and very similar to two examples found at Coddenham (CDD 022) and the other is a Cunobelin. Two pottery kilns were excavated. The pot styles and the stratigraphy indicated that they had been in use during the mid-first century AD with an output including some apparently experimental items in styles resembling first-century pottery produced in Colchester. Triangular loom weights found in the context of the kilns were similar to those recorded at Iron Age sites at West Stow (WSW 002) and Burgh (BUG 002) and the first-century Roman site at Pakenham (PKM 005).

Unfortunately local development has prevented further investigation of the site so the extent of this enclosed settlement is not known, though there were

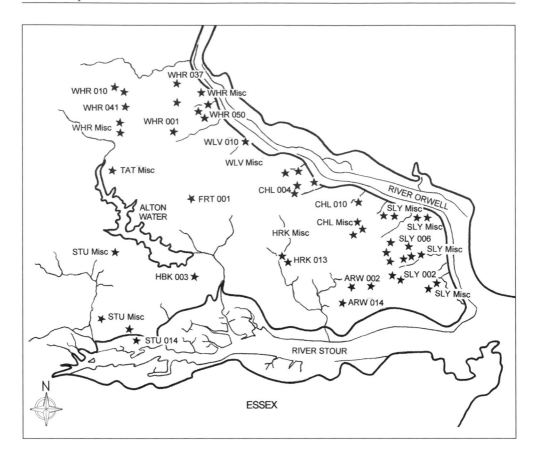

11 Sites map: Roman period. (SMR map redrawn)

indications of movement northwards down the hill during the Roman period. This would have taken the hilltop community to a place-named Camp Yard on the 6in:mile OS map of 1891 and current OS Explorer 197. The field-name camp from ME *camb* 'a bank or ridge of earth', alluding to a local earthwork, fits the local topography admirably.[13] The Bourne Hill ditches could well form part of a complex similar to the later stages of the ditched Iron Age site at Woodham Walters in the Chelmer Valley, Essex and other multi-ditched Thames Valley sites.[14, 15]

Land in the Redgate area of north-west Wherstead has been the source of Roman finds since the nineteenth century (**12**). In 1882 the local vicar F.B. Zincke unearthed more than 1000 sherds of Roman pottery on a clay floor when digging his orchard. The vicarage was less than half-a-mile from the place where a hoard of 2000 Roman coins was uncovered by a ploughman in 1803.[16] The Ipswich Museum's archaeologist Basil Brown (famous for his work at Sutton Hoo) reported finding Roman and Saxon pottery in a pit north of Redgate Lane in 1945;

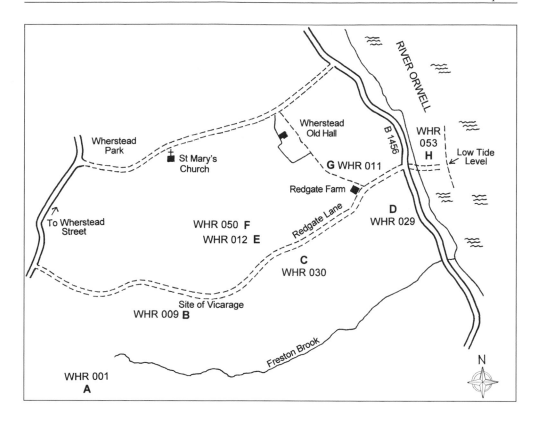

12 Roman period findspots in the Redgate area of Wherstead parish.
A 2000 coins; B 1000 pottery sherds; C, E and F coins and pottery; D undated
enclosure; G Niedermendig lava quernstone; H Redgate Hard

his geologist colleague, Harold Spencer, picked up a piece of Niedermendig lava quern beside the stream that flows towards Redgate Lane from Wherstead Old Hall (WHR 011, 012).

In 1985 aerial photographs revealed a major Romano-British site beside Redgate Lane (WHR 030) (**13a** & **b**) near Zincke's rectory and approximately half-a-mile south-east of Bourne Hill. It was firmly dated by metal detector users. Their initial discovery of a hoard of third-century Roman bronze coins was followed by further finds which included Roman coins (first- to fourth-century) and fragments of two first-century bronze brooches. The site merges into a small plantation on the hilltop and does not appear to extend further south beyond the trees. Its north-facing slope overlooking the Orwell lies roughly within a rectangular area bounded by a ditch on the north-east and a near-vertical embankment which forms the site's south-western boundary. An undated ?Roman enclosure in the field below (**14**), visible on another aerial photograph (WHR 029), appears to include a trackway approximately in line with the hilltop

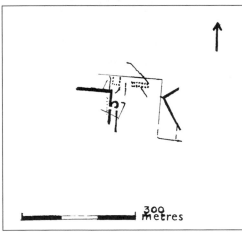

13 a (above) Roman period site beside Redgate Lane in Wherstead parish revealed by aerial photography after a coin hoard was found in the vicinity. Redgate Lane (bottom right corner) is its north-west boundary. (Photograph I. MacMaster)

13 b (left) The existence of a substantial building on the site is indicated by post-hole cropmarks on the north side of the site. (Analysis I. MacMaster)

site, connecting both these sites with Redgate Hard. The Hard (**15**) is defined by a line of posts reaching out into the Orwell. A hard near Pond Hall on the other side of the water, shown on the 1891 edition of the 6in:mile Ordnance Survey, could be the end of a causeway or bridge across the Orwell: OE *brycg* can mean either 'bridge' or 'causeway'.[17] This crossing was named Dunhom Bridge in 1352 when its northern end was a boundary mark of the Liberties of Ipswich.[18] In the sixteenth century the bridge — then named Downham Bridge — had accumulated so much silt that it was a barrier to all but the smaller ships bound for the port of Ipswich.[19] The evidence for this 'bridge' is reviewed by W.G. Arnott in his book about the River Orwell.[20]

14 Aerial photographs taken in 1977 showed this enclosure beside the Orwell River, bounded by Redgate Lane and Wherstead Strand. It is separated from the Roman site (13a) by a straight raised bank. Tracks within the enclosure visible on the photograph point south-west towards the Redgate Roman site. (Photograph SMR)

Downham/Dunhom appears to contain the OE element *hām* 'a village', but there is no trace of a village in the vicinity. In this instance the rarer OE element *hamm* 'river meadow' fits the location, so Downham probably refers to a Saxon site — 'Dunna's riverside meadow', its name derived from the OE personal-name Dunna with OE *hamm*. The aerial photograph (**14**) may show the site of Dunna's meadow, occupying land once part of the Romano-British complex on Redgate Hill. Margaret Gelling discusses the meaning of the OE element *hamm* and the criteria which distinguish it from *ham*, in *Place-names in the Landscape* pp41-50.[21]

Anecdotal evidence of 'squared-off blocks of stone' dredged from the river bed when the shipping channel in the Orwell was deepened in 1951/2 has been interpreted as evidence that the causeway was Roman in origin. The proximity of the Redgate Lane Roman site adds some weight to this idea. Perhaps a causeway

15 Redgate Hard, Wherstead, where a line of posts seen at low tide marks a former causeway crossing the Orwell. It may also have been the site of the wharf that gave Wherstead its name. (Photograph J. King)

was constructed to link Roman Wherstead with the Roman fort and harbour at Walton (Felixstowe). The building indicated by post-holes visible on the aerial photograph of the site (**13b**) might have been used to store grain destined to supply Roman army requirements on the Continent, but if this were so transport by water would have been cheaper. An alternative geological explanation is that the causeway was based on a natural ridge where septaria on the river bed was sufficiently exposed at low water to provide a crossing place. Septaria (and sarsen stones) are frequently brought up by the dredgers employed to maintain the correct depth of the Orwell shipping channel.

The line of substantial wooden posts that march into the river at Redgate Hard may be the remains of a jetty of unknown date, not necessarily connected with the Roman period (WHR 053). This part of Wherstead parish was Wervesteda in 1086 — 'place by a wharf or shore'.[22] Without dating evidence it is impossible to judge how long this jetty may have been in use. It may have originated as a riverine trading base connecting Late Iron Age and Romano-British settlements with Colchester. Local finds of Cunobelin coins would support this idea. It is possible that the wharf may have been made in the seventh/eighth century to serve a post-Roman trading centre or entrepot connected with Gipeswic. It may be significant that the ON word *bryggia* means 'jetty, quay' not 'bridge'[23] which suggests that

16 Cropmarks in a 1975 aerial photograph of Pages Common Field in western Chelmondiston. The dark patches were old gravel pits. A large amount of Roman pottery was found in the north of the field near the cottages (top centre). Roman metalwork has been collected from this area. (Photograph NMR)

Redgate Hard may have been Danish. Systematic survey of this part of Wherstead could be very rewarding.

Elsewhere in Wherstead parish field-names reinforce archaeological evidence suggesting the existence of a Romano-British farmstead near present-day Thor(r)ington Hall. A dense scatter of Roman pottery sherds was found on the top of a south-facing slope west of the Hall (WHR 010). A 1676 plan of the Thorington estate[24] marks a 17-acre field in this same area called Blackamore Lands in 1676 (Blacklands 1968). Where there is additional archaeological

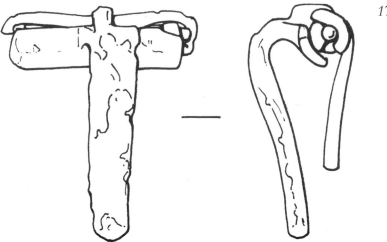

17 A Roman brooch — Colchester derivative — found in the Chelmondiston/ Woolverstone borderland. (Drawing SMR)

18 Part of an aerial photograph taken in the summer drought of 1996 shows a complex of trackways and field boundaries in a field south-east of Woolverstone Hall; some may be related to those shown in 26. Material collected by fieldwalkers and metal detector users, plus the written record, suggest that the Chelmondiston/Woolverstone borderland has been settled and cultivated for more than 1500 years. (Photograph Essex County Council)

19 The Ipswich Metal Detector Club's Shotley Survey was a serious and very successful enterprise. A competition to find tokens hidden in the field near the church provided light relief and welcome funds for several charities. (Photograph D. Palmer)

evidence, 'Black' names are generally accepted as indicators of Roman habitation sites.[25]

Freston parish has not yet yielded any firm evidence of Iron Age or Romano-British settlement though the discovery of a hoard of fourth-century Roman coins in 1959, ploughed up with the remains of two grey-ware pots in which they were probably buried, suggests the existence of activity in the vicinity (FRT 001).

The early history of the land bordering the Orwell between Woolverstone and Chelmondiston is complex. Evidence provided by aerial photographs, field-walking and metal detecting combined with information from documentary sources suggests intermittent occupation from the Late Iron Age into the sixteenth century. Until the Berners' Woolverstone Estate was sold in 1938 parkland occupied most of the parish that lay beside the Orwell. It has been suggested that when the park was established early in the eighteenth century its eastern boundary encroached on Chelmondiston land. In 1726 Knox Ward, the original owner, bought $7\frac{1}{2}$ acres of Woolverstone Field in the western edge of Chelmondiston parish and took them 'within his Park Pale'. This boundary was retained when the Berners family bought the Park. Woolverstone Field is listed in an 1830 schedule of the Berners Estate Lands.[26] Roman metalwork finds from this area, where the present parish boundary zigzags down to the shore, have been recorded as the Chelmondiston sites CHL 004 and 015.

*20 The site of a farm that prospered from the Late Iron Age into the Roman period on land
east of Colton Creek (Shotley parish). The Creek flows into the Orwell (right). Some
of the cropmarks on this photograph may relate to Calu Wetuna (DB), Caluton (20
holdings in c.1380) and Carlton (mid-sixteenth century). (SMR photograph)*

Aerial photographs taken in 1975 show an intricate pattern of trackways and field-systems in a large field that slopes south-east to the main Ipswich-Shotley road (CHL 004) (**16**). Field-walking yielded a scatter of pottery focussed on the cross-way where the medieval Common Way from Woolverstone to Chelmondiston meets a lane of unknown age (Richardsons Lane now) that continues as a footpath towards the Orwell shore to meet a riverside path.

The pottery finds included much Roman material, plus a few sherds of Thetford-type ware and rather more of medieval and post-medieval origin. A metal detector user who explored the surrounding fields discovered Trinovantian coins and a gold stater of the Ambiani dated to 120-100 BC, all in the vicinity of the cross-way. Roman finds from the Woolverstone side of the present parish boundary, close to the cross-way area, include a copper alloy figurine of Mercury, coins dating from the first to the end of the fourth century AD (one an irregular

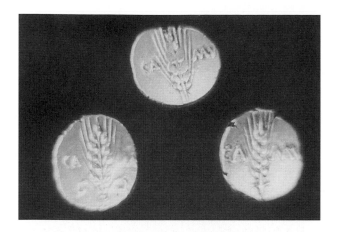

21 Gold staters of Cunobelin, believed to have been part of a small savings hoard buried in a Shotley field near the river Orwell. The ear of corn on the obverse and the single prancing horse on the reverse are defining features of Cunobelin's gold coinage; the initials CUNO indicate that they were minted in Camulodunum, probably in c.AD 30-40. (Photograph J. Newman)

Claudius I) and a bronze bow brooch. Taken together these finds imply Late Iron Age activity continuing into the Roman period, spread over a large area between the Orwell and the present main road, stretching south-west from the borders of modern Chelmondiston up to and beyond its boundary with Woolverstone parish boundary (CHL 004, 016, 017, 028, Misc 13549; WLV 015, 024, 028). Within this area it seems that a Late Iron Age settlement evolved into a Romano-British community most probably living north of the cross-way and farming lands on both the north- and south-facing slopes (**18**). Evidence for later Saxon settlement in the area, suggested by aerial photographs and supported by documentary sources, is presented in chapter 9.

In Shotley parish aerial photography again provided the first intimation of early settlement. One site, in a field between Hares Creek and Colton Creek, was explored by metal detector users between 1980 and 1986 as part of a meticulously planned survey of about a third of the parish, carried out by the Ipswich Metal Detectors Club (**19**). This field (**20**) yielded six gold staters of Cunobelin (**21**). They were scattered on a north-facing slope overlooking the Orwell. Later finds

22 Cropmarks to the west of Colton Creek may be related to the farming activities on its eastern side (20). Colton Creek winds northwards, bottom-right to top-left corner, to flow into the River Orwell. (Photograph Cambridge University Collection of Air Photographs: copyright reserved)

in the same field included other coins of Late Iron Age and early Roman date, a few late Roman coins and part of a copper alloy terret ring. The Cunobelin coins were probably amassed as a savings hoard, buried during the latter stages of Cunobelin's reign.[27] Since these finds were made regular monitoring of the site has led to the discovery of three more Cunobelins in the same area.

This site has been recorded as the farm of a wealthy Iron Age family that continued in Romano-British occupation until late Roman times. A field-walking survey in 1989 failed to locate any pottery sherds in this field but later investigation which included the adjacent field further west, nearer to Colton Creek, yielded sherds of Roman grey-ware and some ?Samian; Mid- to Late Saxon presence was attested by sherds of Ipswich- and Thetford-type wares. The Colton Creek area was recorded as Calu Wetuna in the Domesday Book (DB ii f 295b). Nothing is known about the full extent of this Iron Age farm or of its successors. Cropmarks on the west side of Colton Creek hint at farming activity there (**22**).

Another Romano-British farm in the north-east of the Shotley Peninsula, also on land near a formerly tidal creek, produced no tell-tale cropmarks. Its presence was revealed by metal detector users. On a hill top commanding a fine view over the Orwell estuary and its exit to the North Sea they found several Roman brooches and many Roman coins dating from the second to the late fourth century (SLY 034). A field-walking survey yielded a sherd of Belgic-ware, numerous Roman pottery sherds including Samian, Nene Valley and Oxford-wares plus some roofing tile and a fragment of an amphora. The grey-ware included fragments of storage vessels, jars and bowls. These finds were focussed on the easterly half of the field. Farming operations probably extended westwards into adjacent fields (not yet field-walked) where shadowy cropmarks indicate field systems and trackways. This prosperous farm was occupied until AD 360-75 but abandoned towards the end of the Roman period; no signs of later occupation have been found.

In the central part of Shotley parish, metal detector users found relatively large amounts of Iron Age and Roman material, chiefly in a roughly rectangular area bordered by Church Lane, Old Hall Lane, Shotley Street and the main road to Ipswich. Finds included Iron Age and early Roman coinage. The quantity of material recovered implies the existence of at least one settlement of Iron Age origin, continuing into the Roman period, similar to those already described. A local resident's remark about 'a pile of ancient pottery' seen in a field not far from the church points to a site near a once-tidal creek, typical of known sites elsewhere in the peninsula. An undated rectangular enclosure within a crop-marked area lies to the west of Old Hall Hill, near this creek (SLY 041 and 013).

Aerial photographs of western Shotley show complex field-systems and trackways on the flat farmland south of the village hall (SLY 022, 026, 027) for which no dating evidence has yet been found. These may be associated with finds of a few Roman coins dated to AD 120-138, in an adjacent field (SLY 044). This complex could perhaps form part of a larger site extending into Erwarton parish, where a metal detector user found Roman coins dated from the first to the fourth centuries AD, a bow brooch and a large piece of box tile; cropmarks show a large rectangular enclosure nearby (ARW 014) (**25**).

A series of other undated enclosures seen from the air, which continue through Erwarton and Harkstead, have yet to be investigated. Much of the western end of the peninsula remains to be explored. Very little metal detecting has been carried out on land facing the Stour and no field-walking other than a survey of Stutton.[6] Neither Holbrook nor Stutton parishes have yet provided evidence of settlement in locations similar to those in the rest of the peninsula, though aerial photographs suggest many possible sites in both parishes. A hoard of fourth-century bronze coins found in marshy ground beside the Stour and pottery including Samian and grey-ware unearthed at a building site near the river in 1930 are the only finds in Holbrook parish on record at present (HOL 022, 023).[29]

23a   A Roman lock bolt concealed in an animal form. (Drawing SMR)

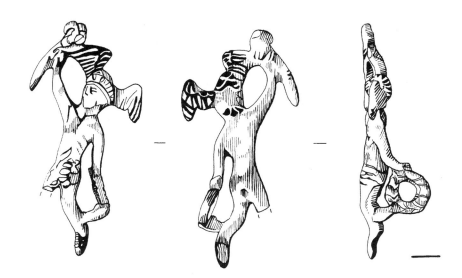

23b   A small bronze figure of Mercury (minus his right leg). (Drawing SMR)

7 The migration period

Early in the fifth century AD the Roman army withdrew from Britain, leaving the newly independent population without the organised systems of local government, communications and trade which had evolved under Roman rule. Archaeological evidence suggests that in the south and east of Suffolk some small towns and farmsteads had already been abandoned by the end of the fourth century. Analysis of SMR data for coin finds throughout the Roman period demonstrates a sharp fall in numbers in non-urban sites between AD 348 and 401 in the southern and eastern parts of the county.[1]

The rural population, though depleted in numbers, continued to live on some of the farmsteads. These predominantly British communities would have included some people of European origin whose forebears had come to Britain with the Roman armies or had been employed as mercenaries in the last years of Roman rule. There would also have been others whose pirate or trading ancestors had settled in eastern coastal regions.

Between the fifth and mid-sixth centuries the situation was changed radically by the influx of Germanic and Scandinavian people who moved into the east and south of Britain (**24**). Formerly described as invasion, this movement is now regarded as migration: some incomers were people whose low-lying homelands were being inundated by rising sea levels and others may have been adventurers attracted by the opportunity of moving into temporarily undefended fertile land where the climate was kinder than on the mainland.

Within a few generations Anglo-Saxon culture was dominant and Old English had replaced the British language. Throughout the preceding Roman period native Britons would have grown used to hearing the Germanic speech of soldiers and other Germanics already living among them, so that the incomers did not impose a new language on the Britons — their presence simply reinforced the use of speech already familiar.

Apparently the people who came to eastern Britain maintained contacts with their home countries. The similarity of metal artefacts found both in Britain and on the Continent implies not only common cultural ideas but also the existence of exchange links between eastern England and the countries of north-western Europe. Whether trading also occurred in the early migration period is uncertain.[2]

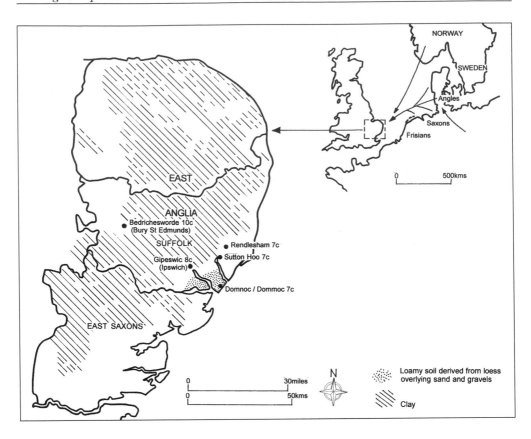

24 Immigrants from north-west Europe came to south-east Suffolk at the end of the Roman period; important settlements were founded before towns evolved. (Modified drawing from An Historical Atlas of Suffolk, *third edition 1999, courtesy Edward Martin)*

At present there are many unanswered questions about the migration period. How long did it last? Was it mainly peaceful or as bloody as Gildas later described it? Did the incomers intermix, displace resident Britons or settle initially on unoccupied land? How many people came? Was intermarriage a factor that may, in part, account for the apparent disappearance of British people in eastern England and their replacement, within a few generations, by a vigorous hybrid population? These questions were discussed at length at the second San Merino Symposium on the Anglo-Saxons; no firm conclusions were reached.[3]

In the Shotley Peninsula no material attributable to the migration period or to the Early Saxon period that followed has yet been found. No pagan cemeteries or burials are known in the area, no pottery sherds have been collected; and, although metal detectors have been used extensively in several parishes over the past 20 years (and most finds reported), no metalwork of the period has been discovered. On present evidence, therefore, it seems that the British population of

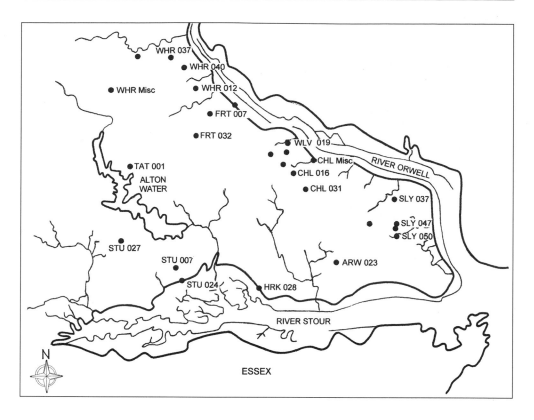

25 The pattern of Saxon sites in the Shotley Peninsula known in AD 2000. (SMR map redrawn)

the Shotley Peninsula remained undisturbed by an influx of migrants. This view, based on very slender, largely negative archaeological evidence, may well have to be modified when more of the peninsula has been investigated. The apparent absence of Early Saxon settlement in the area appears to be confined to the Shotley Peninsula. There are well-attested settlements of the period in the Deben and Gipping valleys, at Walton in the Felixstowe peninsula, and sixth and early seventh-century cemeteries are known in Ipswich.

Whatever the reasons may have been for the apparent absence of Early Saxons, Saxon presence in the Shotley Peninsula became detectable following the widespread introduction of pottery manufactured in Gipeswic from *c*.650 (**25**). Settlement evolution during the years that followed will be outlined in the next chapters, using both archaeological data and place-names.

8 Saxons and Danes: the archaeological record

Pottery

Wheel-made pottery was manufactured in Gipeswic (Ipswich) from *c*.AD 650 until *c*.AD 1150. The products, designed for a variety of uses, were widely distributed. These materials were hard and durable — sherds are easily recognisable after hundreds of years' wear and tear in cultivated fields.

They are generally accepted as dating indicators: Ipswich-ware for the Middle Saxon period *c*.650-850 and Thetford-type ware (so-called because it was first discovered there) for the Late Saxon period (*c*.850-1150). Because of the date range, very late examples of Thetford-ware are often called Saxo-Norman.

None of these types has been found in abundance in the Shotley Peninsula. The small numbers of sherds collected by field-walkers probably result from manurial spread, indicating farming communities in the neighbourhood but giving no exact clues about where people were living. The areas investigated so far include only a very small proportion of the peninsula's arable land. Originally the search was focussed on places where interesting cropmarks had developed during dry summers in the mid-70s. This approach proved more successful in locating prehistoric and Romano-British artefacts than Saxon pottery.

More recent surveys have located small amounts of these wares on farmland in five parishes. The findspots were near the sites of medieval halls: Erwarton Hall, Pannington Hall (Wherstead), Bond Hall (Freston), Woolverstone Old Hall (**26**) and Chelmondiston Manor Hall.

The Woolverstone finds, considered with later finds of medieval pottery in the same general area plus place-name evidence, imply Middle Saxon settlement that developed into a nucleated village. In Chelmondiston parish a single sherd of Thetford-type ware was found near Church Lane in a field west of the site of the former manor hall, where other finds ranged from Iron Age coins to post-medieval pottery. Together these point to a complex pattern of habitation spread over a long period; place-names suggest the existence of a nucleated village centred on the church with open fields on the higher land to the east (p51).

26 *Cropmarks in land formerly part of Woolverstone Park may indicate the site of a Saxon Hall and its associated field systems. The present Woolverstone Hall's water tower (site of the eighteenth-century hall) appears (north) in the top half of the picture. (Photograph Essex County Council)*

Metalwork

Finds of Saxon- and Viking-period metalwork in the peninsula are more abundant than pottery and somewhat more helpful as indicators of potentially interesting sites.

The seventh-century gold pendant (**27**) found near the site of Freston's medieval hall implies the presence of a wealthy high-status owner. Two silver sceattas (**28**) — proto-pennies — dated to the early eighth century, found by a metal detector user in fields near the Woolverstone/Chelmondiston parish boundary within sight of the Orwell, suggest that this could have been a local trading place. These coins are of a relatively high value for the period and probably would not have been used in day-to-day transactions (John Newman, pers comm).

Three metalwork finds indicate later, but not necessarily continuous, Saxon presence nearer to present-day Chelmondiston village: an eight-century sword

27 *This mid-Saxon gold pendant has a central boss of garnet surrounded by filigree decoration of beaded wire in the form of a St Andrew's cross. Found on land near the Orwell shore in Freston parish, it is now in the Ipswich Museum. (Photograph J. Newman)*

28 *A silver sceatt, one of two found in a Woolverstone field near the Orwell in the area illustrated in* **61**. *This 'Kentish' series B-type sceatt, minted c.AD 690-710, perhaps in London, and a series A-type recovered from the same area, are the only sceattas found so far in the Shotley Peninsula. (Photograph J. Newman)*

pommel of gilded base silver (**29**) was found south of the main road through the village, a ninth-century bronze strap-end from a Saxon belt (**30**) was picked up on the Pin Mill foreshore and a cut halfpenny of Aethelred (976-1016) was detected near Church Walk (CHL 031, CHL Misc 10049 and CHL 016). Saxon period materials discovered in other parts of the peninsula are illustrated in **31-4**.

Metal detector users concentrating on the north of Shotley parish found clear evidence of Viking influence in an area west of Old Hall Creek. At that time this

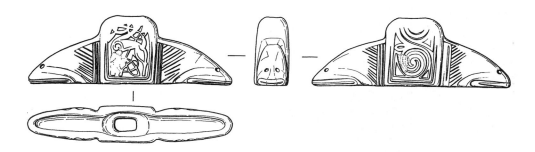

29 This eighth-century sword-pommel made of gilded bronze was found in Chelmondiston parish. The interlace pattern on one side of the central panel may represent an animal or sea-beast; the ends could be animal heads (or sea-beasts) with glaring eyes. (Drawing SMR)

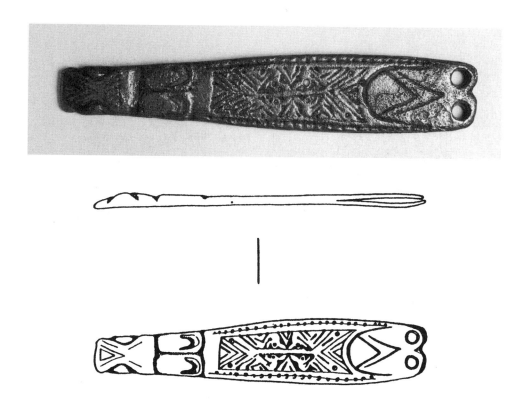

30 This ninth-century strap-end found on the Orwell shore at Pin Mill is in the Ipswich Museum. It is 6.59cm long. The central panel is decorated with a shallow design of punched dots; the terminal is a blunt-ended animal head. (Photograph Ipswich Museum)

31 A caterpillar (ansate) brooch, 4cm long; ninth-century Hubener group 9. It was found in Shotley and is now in the Ipswich museum. (Photograph Ipswich Museum)

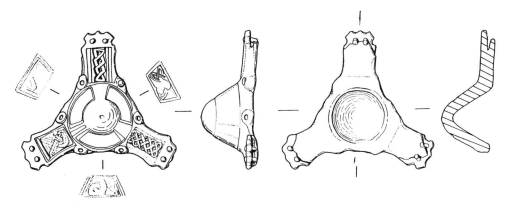

32 A Late-Saxon strap-separator from Erwarton. Made of bronze, it has a hollow centre and three arms each with a different interlace pattern. There are two silver rivets at the ends and at the junction of the arms with the central cone. (Drawing SMR)

creek was tidal, giving access to the Orwell Estuary and the North Sea. Two bronze artefacts found near this creek were decorated in typical Anglo-Scandinavian style. One, a bronze plate decorated with a beast (**35**) — perhaps a horse — in Ringerike style is dated to *c.*AD 1000. It may have been a die used for foil work (SLY 047). Animal-head motifs are displayed on a belt mount and on a diamond-shaped stud (or belt decoration) also found in this area (SLY 050, 053). An eleventh-century bronze brooch (**36**) from a nearby field is decorated with the body of a serpentine animal and interlaced tendrils, in the Urnes (Anglo-Scandinavian) style (SLY 056). Similar metalwork has also been found in the south of the peninsula: a bronze strap-separator (**32**) from Erwarton parish has interlace patterns on its conical centre and three arms and the surface had been gilded and inlaid with silver dots and rivets.[1]

33 Fragment of a
ninth-century
bronze strap-
end: part of
two panels of
niello-inlay
with silver wire
scrolls above
two empty
panels. It was
found in
Stutton parish.
(Drawing
SMR)

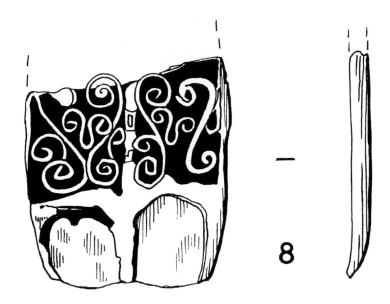

34 A Saxon quatrefoil
strap-separator (one
arm missing) found
on the Stour
foreshore in
Harkstead parish,
enlarged to show
detail: the arms are
decorated with
acanthus foliage. It
was probably made
in the ninth
century. It is in the
Ipswich Museum.
(Photograph
SMR)

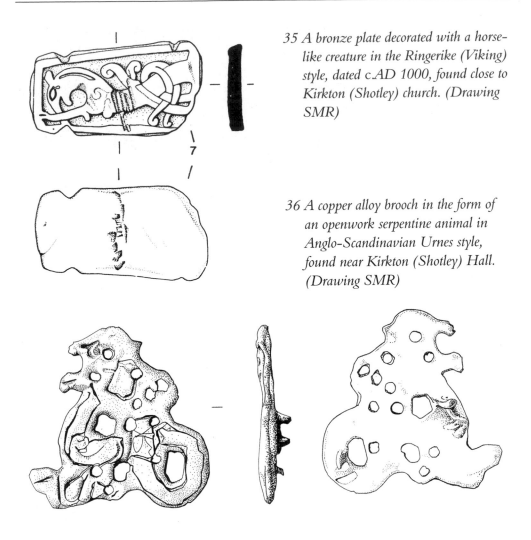

35 A bronze plate decorated with a horse-like creature in the Ringerike (Viking) style, dated c.AD 1000, found close to Kirkton (Shotley) church. (Drawing SMR)

36 A copper alloy brooch in the form of an openwork serpentine animal in Anglo-Scandinavian Urnes style, found near Kirkton (Shotley) Hall. (Drawing SMR)

A fragment of a bronze strap-end (**33**) dated to the ninth/tenth century found in Stutton parish is decorated with niello and curvilinear silver wire. This is recorded as Saxon not Viking (STU 027).

Authentic Viking coins are rare in Suffolk. The silver halfpenny found by chance on the Woolverstone foreshore when the marina was under construction there appeared to be a Saxon coin issued in the late ninth century during King Alfred's reign. It was, in fact, a Viking forgery (WLV Misc 132230).

37 Saxon carved stone incorporated in the outer walls of St Peter's church, Stutton. (Photographs V. Scott)

Carved stone

St Peter's church, Stutton, provides the only known example of Saxon stonework in the peninsula. Carved stone built into the outer wall of the vestry and the south buttress during major rebuilding in the late nineteenth-century has been dated to the tenth/eleventh century (**37**) (STU 007). Its original purpose and location are not known. It may have been part of a grave slab or a cross, from the early graveyard west of the church. This burial ground was unsuspected until bones were unearthed when a new rectory was being built in the nineteenth century. The bones were buried again in an unrecorded grave in the present churchyard.[2] The Mills Manuscripts, held in the village by the Stutton Local History Group, include this account and a number of other antiquarian notes.[2] Two Ipswich-ware pots (**38**) were dug up when the churchyard at Stutton was being extended in 1908. They are now in the Ipswich Museum, one complete and the other reconstructed. Chance finds of sherds of this type of pottery are still being discovered on bare ground in the churchyard and in the area just beyond its northern boundary.[3] Further evidence of Middle Saxon Stutton is attested by the chance discovery of Ipswich-ware sherds on the Stour foreshore only a few hundred yards from the church.

38 Ipswich-ware pots, 18cm high, from Stutton churchyard extension. For many years they were kept in the church vestry; now they are in the Ipswich museum. (Photograph Ipswich Museum)

An earthwork in Holbrook Park

Holbrook Park, formed between the eleventh and twelfth centuries, contains an earthwork that zigzags through the interior of the wood, as if it were the boundary of a pre-existing Saxon wood from which the park was made (**39**).[4]

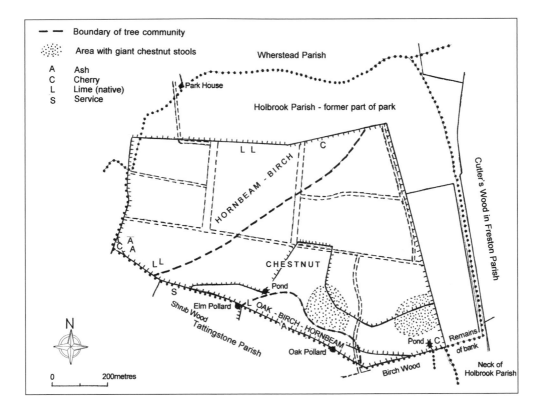

39 A zig-zag earthwork within the wood banks of Holbrook Park, perhaps a relic of Saxon activity pre-dating the Park. (Courtesy Oliver Rackham)

9 Names: sites, settlement, estates

Place-name elements and chronology

The evolution of settlement in the Shotley Peninsula, discernible in the archaeological record, is also reflected in, and in some instances clarified by, the area's place-names. Their value in relation to sites dating from the first 400 years AD has been discussed earlier. For the years following the migration period, local place-names incorporating Old English and, occasionally, Old Norse elements indicate, in broad outline, where settlements were established and how they evolved into the pattern revealed in the Domesday Book. In some instances later documentary evidence helps to locate a settlement more precisely.

Current understanding of place-name chronology allows settlements to be arranged, broadly, in date order. From a study of English place-names in the Midlands and East Anglia containing the element *hām*, Barrie Cox suggested that these names belong to the pagan Anglo-Saxon period *c.*400-650.[1] His later analysis of a large number of place-names collected from the earliest English documents suggested that in the period 400-730 topographical elements important in name-formation included six found in the Shotley Peninsula: *burna*, *dūn*, *feld*, *ford*, *leah* and the habitative element *hām*. However, his conclusions may not be wholly applicable to East Anglian place-names for the region was not represented in his sources.[2] The most recent account of English place-name chronology appears in chapter 7 of Margaret Gelling's *Signposts to the Past*, 1997 edition. She has pointed out that place-name chronology has to be considered separately for each region. The generally accepted view is that the earliest settlement names were topographical, having first elements related to prominent features in the local landscape: hills, rivers and streams. As populations increased and more land was occupied, the local availability of useful natural resources attracted new settlements with names in which a habitative element was qualified by a prefix defining the nature of the resource. Names in which the second element *ingas* is combined with a personal-name refer to territory occupied by the family or followers of that person. Cox found that this type of place-name appears to have been important before 730.

A personal-name combined with the element *tūn* describes an extensive area — an estate — held by the person named. These names could date from the time when the first gifts of land were being made to lay people and probably continued to be coined up to the time of the Conquest.

The *tūn* names, by far the commonest, appear to have been coined over a very long period during which the meaning of tun evolved, as settlements grew in size and complexity, from enclosure to farmstead, then hamlet, village, estate or manor, until eventually it implied town. The meaning of an individual -*tūn* place-name is defined by its first element; dating relies on documentary and archaeological research.

The *hām* names, regarded as comparatively early, generally imply a village. This element can be confused with the topographical term *hamm* which has several different meanings. Only one possible *hamm* has been found among the peninsula's names — Dunhom Bridge (1352) in Wherstead — which probably means 'Dunna's riverside meadow' (p.44).

Place-names containing the element -*stede* meaning 'a place, a locality' are difficult to date.[3]

The Shotley Peninsula's place-names include examples of all these types. Only one — Lopham — contains the element *hām*. Most are *tūns*. Two group names linger in field-names. Both *stedes* and some of the place-names incorporating personal-names became parish names. Most of the personal-names are English; three, perhaps more, are Danish.

Settlement and topography

Climston: a British settlement on a hill slope?

Climston was a place in Harkstead parish, named in the Court and Accounts records of the manor of Harkstead cum Climston (Clymston) between 1413 (the earliest surviving record) and 1565. After that date the name was omitted without explanation. The place also gave rise to a locative surname: John Climes witnessed a quit claim in the late thirteenth century.[4]

Climston held its own courts on the same days as the Harkstead courts. The manor accounts include entries for holdings 'in Climston'. The name appears to have applied to a stretch of land of unknown width sloping southwards from the highest ground in the north of Harkstead (*c*.100ft) to Chapel Down(e) beside the Stour shore. In 1419 a fine was levied 'for removal of the boundary stone from the Lords land 'at Clymston Field'.[5] This field was on the manor's northern boundary. The manor accounts include rents for Climston holdings in Chapel Down — the land in which St Clement's Chapel stood.[6]

The meaning of the word Climston is obscure. The only other examples of the element *clim(s)* occur in the village of Stoke Climsland and a nearby hamlet called Climson, in the Duchy of Cornwall. Ekwall suggests that clim may be a British word related to a hill. Gover also suggested early origin: Climes, Clymes 'an Old Cornish district or hill name'.[7]

If Harkstead's Climston is indeed of Celtic origin then its survival in Suffolk could reflect the late survival of a Romano-British enclave there. So far no evidence of British settlement has been found in the area but there has been very little fieldwork in this parish.

Beria/Bourne: settlement shifting from hilltop to riverside

The place-name Beria (DB ii f 295a) may be derived from OE *byrig*, the dative singular of OE *burh* 'a fortified place, an ancient earthwork'.[8] This is an accurate description of the ditched enclosure at the top of Bourne Hill in Wherstead, described earlier (p41). Though Darby and Versey class Beria in Samford Hundred as unidentified, the topography of the Bourne hill site and details provided in the Domesday Book suggest that the recorder was describing the place that became known as Bourn(e) (1327). Meaning 'place at the spring(s) or stream(s) — as Mills' derivation for Bourn, Cambs and Bourne, Lincs — the name implies early settlement near the River Bourne somewhere in the neighbourhood of present-day Bourne Hill, perhaps on both sides of the river, linked by a ford called Oreford (thirteenth century). This name means ford by the shore or riverbank. A locative surname, de Oreford, appears in Wherstead and Ipswich records. Robert de Oreford of Ipswich witnessed a ?thirteenth-century quit claim relating to land bordered in the south by The Strandweye in Wherstead.[9] Robert de Orford (sic) was an Ipswich Bailiff named in the Portmanmote Rolls in 1280-81.[10] Bourn(e) was first recorded in 1327 when the Manor of Bourne was cited as a boundary in a Wherstead land transaction.[11] It is still in use today: the 1999 $2\frac{1}{2}$in:mile OS Explorer map marks Bourne Hill, Bourne Hall Farm, Bourne Park and Bourne Bridge. In his will (1312) Robert de Reymes left 20s 'for building (? repairing) the bridge at ...'; unfortunately the rest of the word is illegible.[12]

Holton Green (1783): settlement in a shallow valley?

Alton Green in Holbrook parish is a small hamlet with a village green plus a scatter of modern houses and bungalows which spread towards Lower Holbrook. It lies in a shallow valley sheltered by rising ground on the south. It is named Holton Green (**40**) on Hodskinson's map of Suffolk (1793) and on the first edition of the OS 1in:mile map (1838; David and Charles edition 1970). This Green may have originated as an extension of an earlier settlement beside Holbrook Bay. At present there is no evidence to support this suggestion; examination of Holbrook's early manorial records may provide more information.[13] The parish name Holbrook is derived from the OE adjective *hol*, meaning 'lying in a hollow'; in stream names 'running in a deep hollow'.[14] This is

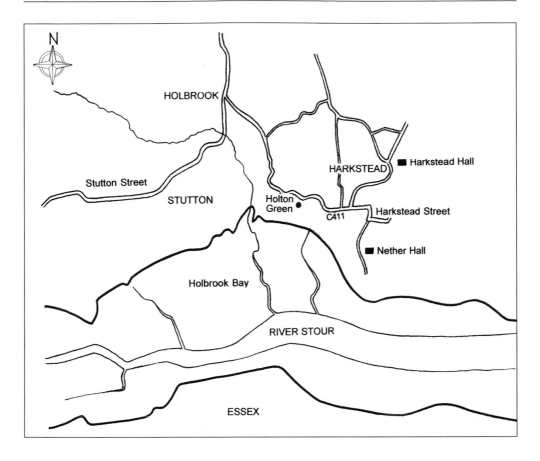

*40 Holton Green in Holbrook parish, perhaps the site of a settlement pre-dating Holbrook
village*

an apt description of the Holbrook stream which runs through the parish into
Holbrook Bay. Its deepest course was dammed to form the Alton Water Reservoir.

Calu Wetuna (DB ii 295b): a hilly settlement

This Domesday vill centred on the head of a creek close to the wealthy Iron Age
farm that remained in occupation into the Roman period (p50). Its topographical
name, meaning 'farm surrounded by bare ground', may be derived from the weak
form of the OE adjective *calewe* 'bare, bald, lacking vegetation', found frequently
in hill names.[15] Mills interprets Calwetone (DB) in Cornwall as 'probably
farmstead by the bare hill'. This description fits the contemporary landscape of
Colton (Calu Wetuna in 1066) in Shotley parish where open heathland lies to the
west and, on the east, there are hilly fields with nineteenth-century names such as
The Downes, Seven Acre Hill and Uplands (Shotley Tithe Map 1839). The
settlement became a medieval hamlet where Wash Lane then marked the tide's

reach. As part of Kirkton manor it flourished in the fourteenth century, declining thereafter until today the only remaining dwellings are Colton Cottage and a former nineteenth-century mill house. Wash Lane is lost in a farm reservoir.

Stuttuna (DB, various spellings): another settlement on a slope
Ekwall offers several alternative interpretations of the Domesday names associated with Stutton parish: 'farmstead or village infested with gnats' (OE *stūt*); 'where bullocks are kept' (ON *stútr*); and 'farmstead by a stumpy hillock' (OE⋆ *stūt*). The topographical interpretation seems the most reasonable.

Downland settlements

Dunton Walton and Curtelisdonlands
Old English *dūn* 'a hill' and Middle English *doun*, 'an expanse of open country', apparently applied to slopes ranging from gentle to mountainous.[16] The first meaning fits areas adjacent to the Orwell in Woolverstone and Chelmondiston parishes.

In the west of Woolverstone parish an ancient hollow way called Dontonstrete in 1491 led to the foot of the impressive earthwork crowning a hilly area called Elbury Down (**41**) overlooking the Orwell (p36). Pasture in this area was called Dunton Walton in 1460 and numerous field-names containing the element dun remained in use into the seventeenth century. This assemblage of names implies settlement in the West Woolverstone Downs dating from the Late Iron Age, continuing as a Romano-British farmstead (Walton) and later as a Saxon settlement remembered as Curtelisdonlands (1460) — ⋆'Cortel's hill lands'.[17] The element *-land* suggests that here, former hill pasture had been converted to arable cultivation.[18] A Middle Saxon dress pin was found on this land above The Cliff in Woolverstone (**42**). The old defended site Elbury still crowns the local downs but no visible trace of the Walton settlement remains.

Chelendelondys: another downland settlement
In the east of Chelmondiston parish a gently sloping tract of land, separated by a cliff from the Orwell shore, lies above the village. Topographically this situation is similar to ⋆Cortel's land above The Cliff in Woolverstone. This part of Chelmondiston was recorded as Chelendelondys and Chelendlondes in the sixteenth century.[19] The OE elements *-ende* and *-land* together mean 'land at the end of an estate'.[20] These names probably refer to Ceolmund's Saxon estate. In 1590 a Common Field in Chelmondiston called Estfeld was conveyed to Thomas Bramston.[21] Its name suggests that the downlands in eastern Chelmondiston had been part of a nucleated village centred on the church and medieval hall. In 1490

41 Elbury Down in Woolverstone Park. A series of sloping banks lead up to an Iron Age defended site occupying the highest ground (top left) hidden by a conifer plantation. (Photograph J. King)

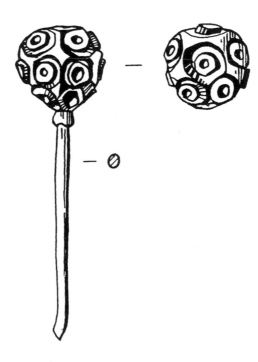

42 A Saxon dress pin made of bronze found in Woolverstone farmland; the lower end of the shaft was missing. The head, which has 17 facets each with a prominent upstanding ring with dot indentation in the centre, sits on a small collar. (Drawing SMR)

the way to the village's Open Fields was Bramston's Lane alias Mowslowe Lane, the steep track that still leads to the farmland from the village.

Lost settlements: Santon and Overton

The complex settlement pattern in north-eastern Woolverstone and north-western Chelmondiston mentioned earlier in the context of the area's archaeology (pp47-9) can be clarified with the aid of two place-names — Chelmondiston Santon and Overton — plus the documentary record.

Santon[22] — 'sandy farm', OE *'sand'* — belonged to the royal township of Chelmondiston when Elizabeth Wolverston held it in soke in the early fifteenth century.[23] Then, it comprised 120 acres of arable land, 20 acres of pasture and 10 of woodland. In 1537 the arable acreage had fallen to 40.[24] The shrinkage is accounted for by a grant of Wolverston manor land to one of its tenants called Runtyng. In 1488 land 'formerly Runtyngs' was held by William Bramston. The name Runtyngs persisted. In 1714, 61 acres 'called Runtyngs' were sold, including fields called Great and Little Sandford and two meadows 'going back into the river' — ie the Orwell.[25] William Berners acquired this land — 65 acres — and took it into Woolverstone Park.

It seems clear that Santon — the sandy farm — once occupied land beside the Orwell in eastern Woolverstone where a sandy ford crossed a stream, perhaps the stream marking the Woolverstone/Chelmondiston parish boundary. The name Santon disappeared from the record in the sixteenth century.

The name Overton, from OE *uferra-tūn* 'higher settlement'[2], points to a settlement which, from other evidence, lay above Santon, in the same area. Its name appeared in the sequence 'Chelmondiston, Overton and Woolverstone (part)' in a schedule of impoverished parishes granted tax reductions in 1428.[27] Apparently Santon and Overton must have been too impoverished to survive for neither name appears in later records.

The name Overton fits a site between Chelmondiston and Woolverstone where medieval and post-medieval pottery sherds have been found in fields lying above those believed to mark the site of Santon (CHL 004) (**43**). Santon was probably the place referred to as 'Woolverstone part' in the 1428 tax assessment. Trackways and field systems visible on aerial photographs of the land that slopes gently down to the Orwell from the common way linking Woolverstone and Chelmondiston churches may well relate to the period when both Santon and Overton were flourishing. Saxon coins — sceattas — found in the Santon area date this settlement to the eighth century AD. Sceattas, coinage in circulation *c.*AD 690-*c.*AD 750, when found (as in Santon) in association with Ipswich-ware (produced between *c.*AD 650-700 and *c.*AD 850), are important indicators of local and inter-regional trading. As yet no Ipswich-ware has been found in the Santon

43 Cropmarks on the upper third of this 1996 aerial photograph of fields in the Chelmondiston/Woolverstone borders may relate to the lost medieval hamlet Overton. The central track is the Chelmondiston/Woolverstone parish boundary (Berners Lane); the large field (right) is part of Pages Common Field; the narrow track (left centre) is the Common Way linking Woolverstone with Chelmondiston. (Photograph Essex County Council)

area, where field-walking is not permitted, but Thetford-type ware has been collected from the higher (Overton) land.

Natural resources
Some settlement sites are associated with useful trees, woodland or mineral deposits

Several names in the peninsula refer to apple, oak and thorn trees. OE *aepell-tun* 'an orchard' is remembered in a Harkstead surname — Roger Apylton was fined for trespass in 1475.[28] In Chelmondiston Thomas Brome conveyed tenements called Apeltons and Salters to William Lemyng in 1599.[29] The Stutton Tithe Map (1844) shows Appleton Field between Samford River and the road to Brantham.

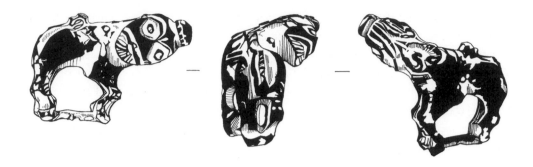

44a *Part of a grotesque copper alloy buckle of medieval date found in a Woolverstone field, formerly part of the lost hamlet of Overton. (SMR drawing)*

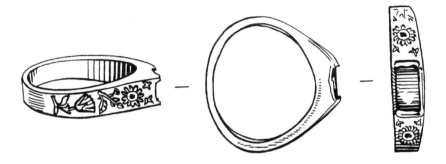

44b *This medieval gold ring (?fourteenth-/fifteenth-century) was found near **44a**. (SMR drawing)*

An oak tree settlement in Harkstead gave rise to a thirteenth-century surname: Elyes de Oakton and Margaret daughter of Alice de Oakton are named in a fine relating to land 'in Herkestede'.[30] This may have become the tenement called Crowsoke (various spellings) in later Court records which include several later references to oak trees. The Sawen Oke was cited as a boundary mark in 1582.[31]

Torintuna (DB ii f 426a) in Wherstead parish was 'thorn tree farmstead' or 'enclosure set within a thorn hedge'. This name, which survives in Thorington Hall Farm, may be related to the Saxon site indicated by pottery finds on one of the farm fields a short distance from the present farmhouse (WHR 010).

Scoteleia: a woodland site

There is no hint of settlement in this name. When the Domesday Survey was made Scoteleia referred only to land at the tip of the Shotley Peninsula — the area now occupied by Over Hall and Rose Farms plus modern housing and land which until recently belonged to the naval training base HMS Ganges. The name

Shotley was not applied to the present parish until the sixteenth century. It was Kirkton before that. The presence of the element -*leah* in the name Scoteleia may be seen as an indicator of woodland in existence when English speakers first arrived in the area. It may be that the tip of the peninsula had become sufficiently depopulated after the Roman period ended to allow unoccupied land to revert to natural woodland. Derivation of the name Scoteleia as 'woodland on a steep slope', from OE *leah* with OE★ *scēot* 'a steep slope', fits the local topography without introducing the pigeons or shooting — OE★ *sc(e)ote* or *sc(e)ot* — usually invoked in interpreting the name.[32] A low-lying field at the foot of the steep northerly boundary of the ex-Ganges territory is called The Hanging, as it was in 1839 (Tithe Map). This field-name is derived from OE *hangra* 'a wood on a steep slope'.

Mineral deposits

Although the peninsula has many deposits of clay, sand and gravel these have not given rise to specific place-names. An exception is Purte pyt (DB ii f 349b), unidentified by Darby and Versey, which appears to have been a pit or quarry in Harkstead, deriving its name from OE (Angl) *pytt* with the OE personal-name Purta. There are no clues about what was in the pit. In 1086 it formed part of a 60 acre manor. Thomas de Pourtepet was a tax assessor in Harkstead in 1327.[33] Harkstead manor records include numerous references to people called Purpette (various spellings) from the fourteenth to the eighteenth centuries.[34] Evidently the land once held by Purta was divided when parish boundaries were drawn, for the lords of Harkstead manor owed suit in Wolverston manor court for Purpette throughout the fifteenth century. In his will (1499) William Tenderyng, then lord of Harkstead manor, directed his executors to 'sell my lands called Purpetts'.[35] The Harkstead and Chelmondiston Tithe Maps show Gravel Pit Fields and Harkstead Clappits lying across their common parish boundary. These may mark the site of Purta's manor.

A wharf

Wervesteda (DB ii ff 295b and 402a) 'place by a wharf or shore' (OE *hwearf* with OE *stede*) gave its name to Wherstead parish. This name holds no clue about where a settlement may have been. The scatter of Saxon pottery found with Roman material near Redgate Lane may be significant. Documentary sources indicate that post-Domesday Wervesteda extended from the Orwell shore — The Strand with its valuable wharf — to high land above the church. This territory included settlements dating from the Late Iron Age and Roman periods to the Saxon estate of Ordgar, known in the thirteenth century as Oregorestun.[36]

Group names and -*stedes*

Group names

Place-names containing the group-name-forming element -*ingas* (genitive plural -*inga*) combined with a personal-name may mean, simply, 'the home or place' of the named person.

Harlings in Shotley may carry the memory of a settlement where the family of ★Herela once lived, or may be interpreted as '★Herela's home or place'. The Harlings was a tenement of the manor of Over and Nether Hall in Shotley in 1729. The Shotley Tithe Map (1839) includes a field called Great Harlings where first-century (?Late Iron Age) pottery was found before the field was built on (SLY Misc 08509). Without earlier versions of this place-name it is impossible to determine whether it referred to a settlement occupied by the family or followers of a man called ★Herela or meant '★Herela's place'. Mills, analysing the name East Harling, Norfolk, which was Herlinge in 1060 and Herlings in 1086, offers either a 'group' interpretation or the singular meaning 'place of a man called ★Herela'.

Painetuna (DB) appears at Paninton (1190), Pamton (1242-3), Painton (late thirteenth century) and Pannington (1528). The name, recalled in present-day Pannington Hall Farm in Wherstead parish, may have been derived from OE *Paegantun* 'Paga's farm' or it may have been an -*ingtun* name[37] (M. Gelling, pers. comm.).

One other possible group place-name in Shotley parish links the OE personal-name Cola with OE *wer*, *waer*, 'a fishing enclosure'.[38] Local names ranging from Collingwere, a croft in Kirkton manor in the 1380s, to present-day Collimer Point, where the course of the Orwell turns sharply southwards, place Cola's settlement of fishermen at a site close to the Orwell shore where the Shotley Tithe Map marks fields called Upper, Middle and Lower Collimer. Long before the river wall was built, this area would have been open to the tides as in Essex, where an array of post-holes in Collins Creek in the Blackwater estuary, revealed by aerial photography, has been interpreted as a massive Anglo-Saxon fish weir; radio-carbon analysis suggests use between AD 600 and 950 (**45**).[39] There are no post-holes visible in vertical aerial photographs of the Collingwere area, held in the National Monuments Record Centre in Swindon; evidence of Cola's weirs may lie within the river embankment.

A second Saxon settlement may have existed in the same area near present-day Mans Cliff, west of Collimer Point. Mondes, a 1561 tenement, and the field-names Munds and Great Munns (Tithe Map 1839) may contain the Saxon personal-name Mann. Alternatively, they may be derived from OE *mann*, *monn* or ON *maðr* 'a man' which gives *manna* in the plural. Cropmarks on aerial photographs indicate settlement in this area, which in the ninth century was associated with the estate of a Dane called Thurketil (SLY023, NMR 826/352).

45 Cropmarks in the fields south of Man's Cliff wood in Shotley parish indicate the site of Cola's fishing weir: the Orwell is visible (top right) beyond the marshland and the river wall. Evidence of Roman activity has been found in this area, which became part of a Danish estate in the ninth century. (Photograph NMR)

Archaeological fieldwork in progress indicates activity in the Romano-British and possibly earlier periods.

The -stedes
Two of the peninsula's Domesday villas, Wervesteda (DB ii ff 295b and 402a), and Herchesteda (DB ii ff 386b, 402b, 430b) contain the element *-stede*.

Wervesteda — 'place by a wharf or shore' — gave its name to Wherstead parish. Documentary sources indicate that Wervesteda extended from the Orwell shore (The Strand) in the vicinity of Wherstead Old Hall to high land above the church.

This territory included settlements dating from the Late Iron Age and Roman periods, and also a Saxon estate — Ordgar's estate — known from a thirteenth-century source as Oregorestun.[40] The scatter of Saxon pottery found with Roman material near Redgate Lane may be significant (WHR 012).

Herchesteda — Hereca's place — gave its name to Harkstead parish.

Estates — X's *tuns*

The first farmsteads established in the migration period probably differed little from those remaining after the Roman withdrawal. As the population grew, new settlements were founded, recognisable by place-names combining habitative and topographical elements. How they were related to the emerging East Anglian Kingdom is not known.

From the seventh century the pattern of land tenure changed. Grants of land to be held 'for ever' were made to newly-established religious foundations and, in the eight and ninth centuries, such grants were also being made to laymen whose names became attached to the territories concerned. Generally referred to as X's *tūns*, X being the holder's name, these estates covered large tracts of land and included all the settlements already existing within them. The emergence of estates marked an important stage in settlement evolution. In East Anglia it is impossible to be sure that the personal-name attached to a specific estate recorded in 1086 was that of the original holder: charters which would have recorded early grants were destroyed in Viking raids. The personal-names revealed by the Domesday Survey simply record the situation at that time — they do not necessarily point to earlier settlements. Nor is it wise to conclude, without more evidence, that parish boundaries indicate the extent of any of these estates.

In the Shotley Peninsula five parishes — Chelmondiston, Erwarton, Freston, Harkstead and Woolverstone — derived their names from estates. Two estates — Caketon and Oregorestun — had no lasting effect on the peninsula's place-name record. Two others — Thurketelton and Brandeston — bear the names of Danish landholders.

Ceolmund's estate, recorded as Ceolmundestun in 1174 (Pipe Rolls) but not named in the Domesday Book, evolved into Chelmondiston parish. Complex reasons have been advanced for linking Ceolmund's tun with the 'unidentified' Domesday entries Canapetuna and Canepetuna (DB ii f 296a, 418b). Siward, who held 20 acres in Canapetuna, also held 6 carucates in Stigand's manor in Hintlesham (DB ii f 289a) recorded as including a salthouse. The latter seems more likely to have been on the Orwell shore at Chelmondiston than in landlocked Hintlesham. Chelmondiston, as a berewick of Hintlesham, would have been assessed for tax with the latter and so not recorded in the Domesday Survey. The £12 increase in Hintlesham's value between 1066 and 1086 could have been Chelmondiston's contribution. Early settlements associated with Ceolmund's estate were Santon and Overton.

Chelmondiston became the royal township of Saunford (Samford) Hundred after the Conquest. How and when this status was achieved is not clear. A translation of The Lord's Rental for Saunford Hundred (undated, probably late fourteenth-century), included as chapter 13, shows how settlement in the Shotley Peninsula and the rest of the Hundred evolved after the Norman Conquest.

Freston parish evolved from Domesday Fresetuna, Frisetuna, 'the estate of the Frisian, Fresa'. How this estate was related to Aelfflaed's pre-Domesday estate in Freston (p.32) is not known. At present there is no information available that could point to early settlement sites within this parish. No early manorial records have survived. The cartulary of the Priory of Saints Peter and Paul, Ipswich, to be published in the Charter Series of the Suffolk Records Society, is expected to include useful information about early place-names in Freston which should provide insight into the early history of the parish.

Hereca's place — Herchesteda in 1086 — gave Harkstead parish its name. Hereca is recorded as an eighth-century OE personal-name (M. Gelling, pers comm). Sandred, who made an exhaustive study of the element *-stede*, considered that its presence in a place-name denotes considerable antiquity.[41] Settlement names associated with Harkstead include Climston, which may date back to the Romano-British period (p67), Oketon and Purte pyt (pp74-5).

Brandeston — the estate of a Danish man called Brand — was also located in the area that became Harkstead parish. There is documentary evidence that places Brandeston below the watershed between Harkstead and Chelmondiston: a conveyance by Martin de Brantestun of a piece of aldergrove 'in Brandeston' states that it was bounded by a watercourse.[42] A quitclaim by Cecilia, former wife of Luke de Brandiston, refers to 'all lands formerly of Luke Brandiston in Chelmondiston and Brandeston'.[43]

The surname Brandeston, also recorded as Bramston or Brampston, is well attested in Chelmondiston, Woolverstone and elsewhere in the peninsula up to the sixteenth century; few references occur in Harkstead's manorial records.

A Brandeston Hall was acquired by Roger Bavent in 1338. After his death in 1350 all his lands were escheated to the Crown and in 1355 granted by Edward III to the newly founded Dominican Priory of Nuns in Dartford, Kent. At the Dissolution they were sold to Sir Percival Harte.[44] There is no reference to Harkstead land in Sir Percival's will.[45] Presumably he disposed of his Brandeston estate before he died. The Harte-Dike family papers in the Kent Record Office probably include relevant details. If not, Brand's estate is effectively lost.

Wulfhere's estate became the parish of Woolverstone. No hard evidence of settlement in the sheltered valley below Woolverstone church has been found but the name Lopham was associated with the area from 1086, when the de Lopham family held the advowson of St Michael's church[46] until 1749 when William Berners bought a messuage in Woolverstone called Lophams. Lopymfeld (1348) was one of the Open Fields belonging to the nucleated village (or hamlet) that developed in the vicinity of the church. Pottery finds near the church and the site of the Old Hall include both Ipswich- and Thetford-type wares; medieval pottery sherds have been found further east. These finds plus the documentary evidence point to a Saxon settlement (Loppa's) later absorbed into Wulfhere's estate, which also subsumed other settlements including Elbury, Dunton Walton, *Cortel's land in the west of the present parish and perhaps also part of Santon in the east. Cropmarks on aerial photographs suggest where Lopham may have been (WLV 012).

Erwarton parish evolved from the estate of a man called *Eoforweard (Mills). The Domesday Survey records two holdings in this area: Eurewardestuna (DB ii f.395a) of 60 acres and Alwartuna (DB ii f.394b), a substantial holding comprising $1\frac{1}{2}$ carucates of land, with a working population of 12 and assets valued at 40s, including a third of a fishpond. In error, the Domesday scribe attributed the former to Thuri, a thegn of the King, and the latter to a free man called Ailbern. The spring-fed farm reservoir in the grounds of Erwarton Hall probably marks the site of the Domesday fishpond in Eure Wardestuna. Confusion between the names Erwarton and Alwarton has persisted ever since.

Almost all the early spellings point to Erwarton as the major settlement name. Three thirteenth-century surnames — Aldewarthon, Aldwartoun and Aldwarton — imply that the second Domesday holding also continued, as a separate settlement.[47] In 1376 Everwarton manor included Thorpe Hall and a tenement called Aldwarton Halle.[48] In later records both Erwarton and Arwarton are used; both appear on a current Ordnance Survey map which names Arwarton Parish, Erwarton Ness and Bay, Erwarton Walk connecting Arwarton Hall (a private house) with Erwarton Home Farm. This map names the ancient manor house as Erwarton Hall.[49] In fact the official name of the parish, today, is Erwarton, pronounced locally with a long A.

It seems that there were two Saxon estates in this parish. The second — Alwartuna — may be interpreted as 'the estate of a man called Aelfweard or Aethelward' (G. Fellows-Jensen, pers comm). Alternatively, it may have been 'the old watch farm', deriving its name from OE element *ald* 'old' (present in Aldewarthon 1209, Aldwartoun 1280 and Aldwarton 1296) with either OE *weard* or the cognate ON *varði*, both meaning 'watch, ward, protection'.[50] Derivation from ON *varði* would reflect local Danish influence. Settlements in the Erwarton/Arwarton area included the Danish Thorp and places called The Hamlett of Walton (sixteenth century) and Walton Common (seventeenth century), indicating the earlier existence of either a British settlement or a walled farm.[51]

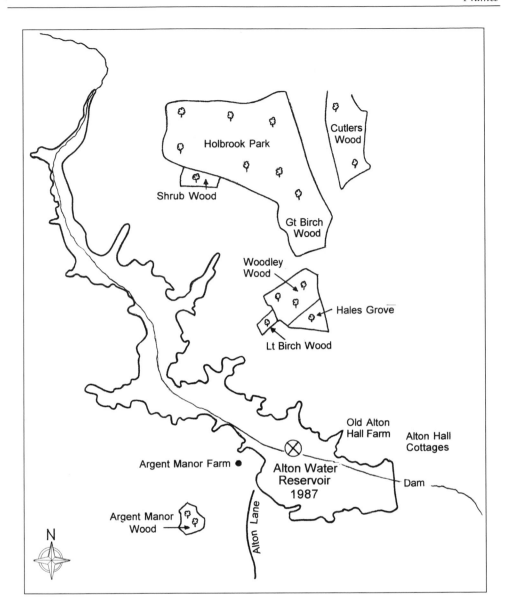

46 Alton Hall lies under Alton Water Reservoir; it may mark the site of the lost DB manor Alfildestuna

Other estates in the Shotley Peninsula

Alfildestuna (DB ii ff 378a, 420a) — the estate of a Saxon woman called ?Aelflaed or perhaps a Danish woman called Alfhild — was unidentified by Darby and Versey. It probably became the medieval manor and later modern estate of Alton Hall in Holbrook parish. Most is now lost under Alton Water Reservoir.

47 This ancient bridleway in the valley of the Holbrook stream was one of many old routes lost beneath the Alton Water Reservoir. (Photograph P. Willis)

In the thirteenth century 'the path from Alton' was cited as the southern boundary of four acres in Holebroch.[52] The southern end of Alton Lane emerges from Alton Water and continues, still, into Stutton village. In 1275 Thomas de Freston held land in Alton and in 1319 John de Freston was granted free warren there. The 1327 Subsidy Return for Holebrok names William, Matthew and Robert 'de Altone'.[53] Modern maps show Alton Hall Farm and Alton Hall Cottages in Holbrook parish on the eastern edge of Alton Water.

Caketon — Cafca's estate — apparently occupied a stretch of heathland in the centre of the peninsula, perhaps granted when more favourable land was in short supply. As Caketon or Kaketon it was recorded in Harkestead, Holbrook, Chelmondiston, Shotley and Woolverstone parishes from the fourteenth century until, in the sixteenth century, references cease. Caketon was common grazing ground in 1348.[54] In 1419 it was one of Elizabeth Wolverston's many holdings, with belongings in Chelmondiston, Harkstead and Holbrook.[55] In the fifteenth century the tenant of Caketon Hall owed suit in the Harkstead Court.[56] As a surname Kaketon and Caketon occur in Shotley Peninsula records from the thirteenth to the fifteenth century: Blaise de Kaketon and Elias (Ellis) de Kaketon witnessed thirteenth-century deeds.[57] Elias de Haketon (sic) is named in the 1327 Subsidy Returns for Holbrook.[58] Robert Kaketon was a tenant in Shotley in 1410[59] and another Robert (Caketon) held land 'in Kyrketon' in 1431.[60] From the sixteenth century the name no longer appears in the documentary record.

Oregorestun — Ordgar's estate — was in Wherstead parish. Fourteenth-century deeds show that an area bounded on the north by The Strand (the Orwell shore) included Oregoretun(e) Strete (Street), numerous Oregoreston crofts, fields and ways, and several boundary 'walls' which may have been relics of an enclosure — perhaps an Iron Age settlement (**14**, p42). Though there is no evidence to support the suggestion, Ordgar's estate may have been the place-named in the Domesday Book as Wervesteda 'the place by the shore with a wharf'; it is possible that present-day Wherstead Street was the site of Oregoreston Street. Robert de Goreston witnessed the lease of tenements in Wherstead, Ipswich, Cauldwell and Westerfield in 1270.[61] Between 1281 and 1388 land 'in Oregoreston' and a street called (in various spellings) Organston Street were named in transactions involving land, a croft and a cottage; all in Wherstead.[62] Analysis of the names of fields and tenements found in Wherstead's

48 This vertical aerial photograph of Shotley parish, south of Collimer Point, taken in 1963, includes the site of Thurketil's Danish estate centred on present-day Shotley Hall Farm, bounded on the north by marshland — River Orwell is visible beyond the river wall. Kirkton (now Shotley) church and hall appear further south, beside present-day Church Lane (lower centre and right). (Photograph NMR)

manorial records,[63] considered together with those recorded as being in or related to Oregoreston, strongly suggest settlement continuity.

That Wherstead became the parish name reflects the economic importance of the wharf beside the Orwell. The parish includes the DB settlements Wervesteda, Painetuna, Torintuna and the riverside settlement Bourn(e) — DB Beria.

Turchetlestuna (DB ii f 420a), 'the estate of a Dane called Thurketil', was in Kirkton (**48**). Since the Domesday name contains the uncontracted form of this Scandinavian personal-name, the estate must have been established before *c*.1000 when the contracted form of personal-names in -ketil began to evolve in the Danish homelands. This indicates that the grant was made in the 880s, in Guthrum's reign (G. Fellows-Jensen, pers. comm.). Turchetlestuna became the eighteenth-century manor of Thurkelton and, as the place-name records show, eventually part of a modern farming estate in the Shotley Peninsula.

In 1240 Godwin son of Geoffrey transferred arable land 'in Thirkeltun and Kyrketune' to William son of Robert.[64] A thirteenth-century fine refers to Thurkelton juxta Kirketon.[65] This name persisted, in various spelling, until in 1746 James Sewell sought Counsel's opinion before buying 'the manor of Thurkelton'.[66] As Kirkolton alias Thurkolton the land was inherited in 1756 by James Sewell's son James. Thereafter the estate acquired other names. It was Carlton Farm in 1758 and Shotley Low Farm in 1838.[67-8] Frederick Schreiber was named as the landowner (345 acres) in 1838 (Shotley Tithe Map). From 1839 it was part of the Berners Estate, sold (363 acres) at auction in 1958 when estate was broken up.[69] Since then Thurketil's land has been part of the Shotley Hall Estate. The territory granted to Thurketil would have included the earlier settlements of Cola and Mann, possibly also Calu Wetuna (Colton).

10 The Danish and Anglo-Scandinavian years

Evidence provided by place-names and by metalwork finds indicates substantial Danish influence in the east and south of the Shotley Peninsula dating from the arrival of Guthrum and his army in AD 880 when East Anglia became part of the territory under Danish rule (**49**). Turchetlestuna was founded in the late ninth century adjacent to the Danish settlement called Kirkton in territory belonging to an existing Saxon village with a church. The spelling Cherchetuna in the Domesday Book may reflect Norman pronunciation of the Danish name. Both Kirkton and Cherchetuna mean 'church village': ON *kirkja*, OE *cirice*, ME *chirche*, 'church'.[1] Kirkton (Kirketon) remained as the name of a manor; later, Shotley was adopted as the parish name. Few traces of Saxon activity have been found in the vicinity of Shotley church but metalwork recovered nearby attests to the Anglo-Scandinavian character of eleventh-century Kirkton, hinting at continuing contact with the Scandinavian homelands.

It seems that the Danish settlers prospered sufficiently to take in adjacent land where a dependent settlement, Torp, was established. Other names indicate Danish penetration further westward on the Stour side of the peninsula at least as far as Harkstead. How much further west their influence reached is not known — documentary sources for Holbrook and Stutton have not yet been examined — but it is clear that names in the Shotley Peninsula, generated during the Danish and Anglo-Scandinavian years, remained in use for hundreds of years after the Norman Conquest.

The major Danish settlements: Kirkton and Thorp(e)

Kirk(e)ton in the Shotley Peninsula is recorded as Cherchetuna in the Domesday Book (DB ii f 395a); Kirkton in the Felixstowe peninsula was Kirketuna in 1086 (DB ii ff 430b, 342b, 423b). In subsequent records both places appeared as Kirton or Kirk(e)ton until, in the sixteenth century, ambiguity was avoided by using 'Kirkton alias Shotley'. By the seventeenth century Shotley had become the accepted name for the whole parish but Kyrk(e)ton continued as the name of an

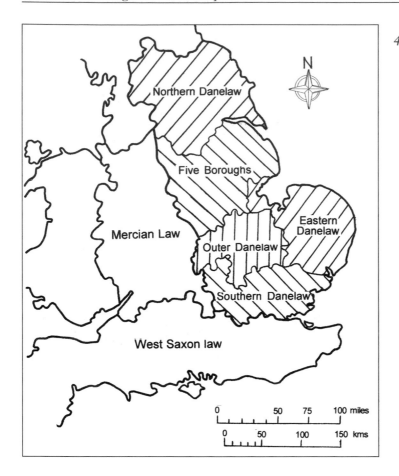

49 The Danelaw, where danish law was observed from the late ninth century until the territory was reclaimed by the English King, Edward the Elder. (Courtesy Cyril Hart)

extensive manor. A rental of *c.*1380 lists 72 holdings, in Kyrketon itself and in Thurkelton (DB Turchetletuna), Caluton (DB Calu Wetuna), Chelmyngton, the Hamlett of Schotlee, Edwarton and 'a close next to Herkestede marsh'. The Chelmyngton land would have been the western part of Calu Wetuna before the Shotley/Chelmondiston parish boundary was drawn through the middle of Colton Creek.[2]

Torp (DB ii f 394b) became Richard de Clare's land in 1086. It was recorded as a 100-acre manor in Samford Hundred, unidentified by Darby and Versey but traceable through the documentary records of Kirkton, Erwarton and Shotley. It occupied an area south of Kirkton, extending westwards into land that belonged to the Saxon estate named Eure Wardestuna in 1066, which is now part of Erwarton parish.

The southerly part of Torp became part of the manor of Shotley Over Hall (**50**). In 1198 two carucates 'in Thorp' were sold by Beatrix and Margaret de Corp (sic) to Walkelin Visdelou, then lord of Shotley Over Hall manor.[3] Thorpe Close was part of the land held in 1624 by Sir Henry Felton, lord of the manor of Shotley Over Hall.[4]

50 Fields belonging to Shotley Over Hall. Land in this area became part of Danish Thorp. (Photograph I. MacMaster)

Thorp lands in Erwarton parish are named in the manorial records of both Kirkton and Erwarton. Jolixnes 'in Thorpecroft in Edwarton' was held of Kirkton manor by Peter Hardekyn in 1380. Thorp as part of Erwarton manor is evidenced from 1327 when John de Thorp was included in the Erwarton Subsidy Return.[5] In 1376 Thorpe Halle was a tenement of Everwarton manor.[6]

Erwarton's manorial records of the seventeenth and eighteenth centuries record numerous Thorpe names: Close, Croft, Meadow, a Shelfe Piece in Thorpe Hall Close and numerous weyes.[7] From a detailed analysis of these records it may be possible to map the area that the Danes called Torp more precisely than suggested in **53**.

How Alwartuna (DB ii f 394b) fits into this account of Danish activity in the area that became Erwarton parish is not clear. Alwartuna contains the OE element *weard* cognate with ON *varði*, both meaning 'watch, ward, protection'[8], suggesting that land belonging originally to a Saxon settlement was occupied, later, by Danes. There is no archaeological evidence to support this idea. The present-day hamlet called Shop Corner, in Erwarton parish, stands on high ground with a superb view over the Stour estuary and Erwarton Creek (**51**) — a perfect site from which

51 The waterlogged marshy land (top right) between low cliffs on the Stour foreshore was once the entry of Erwarton Creek. Its tidal waters originally reached inland as far as Rat Bridge. This is the view over low-lying arable land, seen from the Shop Corner footpath where it drops from c.80ft, suddenly and steeply, towards the south-west. This viewpoint may have been the site of the Saxon look-out at Alwarton. (Photograph J. King)

to keep watch over the water. Who the watchers may have been and when and why they kept a lookout are open questions.

Danish presence further west in an established Saxon settlement can be deduced from the name of woodland in Harkstead parish that retained the Danish version of its original English name long after the Norman Conquest. In 1429 it was 'the lord's wood called Skaldefen'; in 1568 it was recorded as Skalde Fenn Wood.[9] Its English name, derived from two OE words *sceld* 'a shield, shelter' and *fenn* 'a fen, a marsh, marshy ground', described woodland giving shelter to a marshy place. When Danish speakers were living in the area they used their own form of the name — Skaldefen — in which the English soft sh sound was replaced by the Scandinavian hard k. Skaldefen is recorded as a surname in fourteenth-century Thurketelton.[10] Kason Wood (Harkstead Tithe Map 1839) stands on a north-facing slope on the Erwarton/Harkstead parish boundary above damp meadowland; its name contains the ME element *kers* 'a fen'. This woodland, which is still there, may be a relic of Skaldefen Wood: the meadow would have been marshland before Erwarton Creek was dammed (**52**).

52 Erwarton Creek and River Stour in 1971. The minor road C411 meanders from the high land at Shop Corner (right) steeply down to Rat Bridge to cross the stream feeding the Creek, then loops west and north towards Harkstead Street. The low-lying U-shaped meadow below the hanging woods north of Shop Corner may mark the site of Skaldfen. This vertical aerial photograph includes the site of St Clements Chapel (centre, in the corner of a field, close to the river); also the enclosure site (9) further west. (Photograph NMR)

At present, neither archaeology nor place-names provide enough evidence to define more precisely the territory occupied by Danes and Anglo-Scandinavians in the Shotley Peninsula (**53**). It seems to have extended westwards into Harkstead parish, beyond the boundary stream which flows into the Stour via the formerly tidal Erwarton Creek. This creek would have provided a sheltered harbour with excellent access to Danish occupied territory.

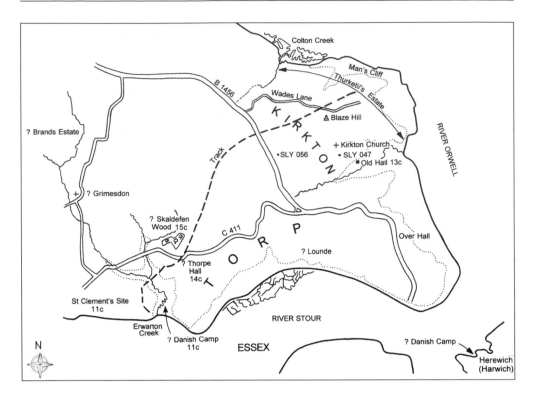

53 Danish influence in the Shotley Peninsula evidenced by place-names. The dotted line indicates the present-day 5m contour.

A Danish (Viking) camp?

Denewall, a lane (venella) named in the 1380 Kirkton rental, may point back to a Danish defensive wall or camp: OE *wall* with OE *Dene* 'the Danes'.[11] This lane was the boundary of a holding close to the stream that flows out of Erwarton Creek into the Stour. Material evidence of an earthwork in the vicinity of this creek may now lie below the Stour's high tide level. Within the last forty years much of the Stour's salt marsh has been lost and erosion is still continuing where — as at Erwarton Creek — the land is unprotected by river walls.[12] Erosion there is not a recent phenomenon. The Harkstead manor accounts for 1448 record the loss of creek marshland worth xiid per annum 'devastated by the sea'.[13]

Danish personal-names

Thurketil is not the only ON personal-name occurring in Shotley place-names. Two — Brand and Grim — were associated with places in northern Harkstead.

Brand's estate and the areas in which his descendants have been recorded were discussed in detail earlier. Unlike Thurketil, Brand's name offers no clue about when the estate was established. It may have been granted in Guthrum's time or acquired in the eleventh century during Cnut's reign. The personal-name Grim occurred in Grimesdon (1206) in Harkstead.[14] It could have been either English or Scandinavian in origin. ON Grímr was a common personal-name in the Danelaw. OE Grim was a by-name of the god Woden, derived from ON *grímr* 'a masked person, one who conceals his identity' — something that Woden was reputed to do. In 1206 Grimesdon was a 40-acre piece of land in Herkested conveyed to Ranulf Bretun by William Pesel. Later it became part of a farm occupying territory on the borders of the three parishes, Harkstead, Chelmondiston and Woolverstone, recorded as part of the Berners Estate in 1789.[15] Harkstead Church stands on the highest ground in the parish. Perhaps it was built on a pagan site once devoted to worship of the Norse god Woden.[16]

A shadowy character called Finn(r) the Dane appears to have been an agent acquiring land on behalf of King William. He held land in five Suffolk Hundreds between 1066 and 1086 which, with that held by Wihtgar, formed the nucleus of Richard Fitzgilbert's Honour of Clare. Finn's land included two carucates 'in Alwartuna' held by Thuri, a king's thegn in 1066.[17]

Gillian Fellows-Jensen has pointed out that people with Danish personal-names were not necessarily actual Danes: it may have been fashionable for English parents to give their children Danish names.[18] The personal-names of the men and women in the Shotley Peninsula recorded in 1066 cannot indicate their nationality but they do point back to the national origin of the individual names.

★ I am indebted to Dr Fellows-Jensen for the following analyses.

Personal-names in the Shotley Peninsula Domesday vills: national origins★

Alfildestuna	Alfhild (feminine) Scandinavian; ?Alwin OE
Alwartuna	Thuri Scandinavian, short form of names in Thor-
Beria	Edeva here and elsewhere OE Eadgifu
Calu Wetuna	Thurstan anglicised form of Scandinavian Thorstein
Canapetuna	Siward either OE or Scandinavian; Brunwin OE
Churchetuna	Edmund OE, Strangwulf OE or ContGerman;
	Thuri Scandinavian, Hun OE Hun or Scandinavian Huni
Eure Wardestuna	Ailbern OE Aethelbeorn
Fresetuna	Robert ContGerman, Wymarc Breton
Herchesteda	Harold Scandinavian, Aelfric and Edeva (Eadgifu) OE

Holebroc	Godman OE
Painetuna	Thurstan Scandinavian; Robert ContGerman
Purte pyt	Osbern probably OE but possibly anglicised Scandinavian or ContGerman
Scoteleia	Wulfnoth, Estmund, Aelfric, Wihtric, Aelfgeat and Ceolwold, all probably OE, Gyrth, Harald and possibly Mann Scandinavian
Stottuna	Edwin and Ednoth OE, Fridebern Cont. German, Scalpi Scandinavian perhaps from the word *skalpr* meaning 'leather sheath'
Torintuna	Alwin OE
Torp	Osbern, probably OE but possibly anglicised Scandinavian or ContGerman
Turchetlestuna	Grim almost certainly Scandinavian
Uluerestuna	Thurstan Scandinavian; Alfred OE
Weruesteda	Edmund OE, Toli Scandinavian, short form of names in Thorl-

Land-holders in the Shotley Peninsula in 1066★

Alfred	(patron Scalpi, Uluerestuna)
Aelfric	free man (patron Harold, Scoteleia)
	free man (un-named patron, Herchesteda)
Aelfgeat	free man (patron Gyrth, Scoteleia)
Aelfric	free man (Scoteleia);
	patron of Osbern (Torp) and Alwin (Alfildestuna)
Ailbern	free man (Eure Wardestuna — ie Alwartuna)
Alwin	free man (patron Aelfric, Alfildestuna)
Alwold	free man (Alfildestuna)
Brunwin	free man of King's manor Bergholt
Ceolwold	(patron Aelfric, Scoteleia)
Eadgifu	Edeva (Beria, Herchesteda)
Edmund	free man (Cherchetuna)
	free man (patron Robert son of Wymarc, Weruesteda)
Ednoth	free man (patron unnamed, Stottuna)
Edwin	free man (Stottuna)
Estmund	free man (patron Harold, Scoteleia)
Fridebern	king's thegn (Scottuna)
Godman	free man (patron Eadgifu, Holebroc)
Grim	free man (patron Earl Gyrth)

Harold	King (Herchesteda)
Hodric	free man (Cherchetuna)
Hun	free man (Cherchetuna)
Osbern	free man (patron Aelfric, Purte pyt and Torp)
Robert	son of Wymarc (Frisetuna and Painetuna)
Robert	(Painetuna)
Scalpi	King's thegn (Stotuna)
Siward	free man (patron Stigand)
Strangwulf	free man (Cherchetuna)
Toli	free man (patron Robert, Wervesteda)
Thuri	king's thegn (Alwartuna ie Eure Wardestuna)
Thuri	free man (patron Gyrth, Cherchetuna)
Thurstan	?free man (patron Eadgifu, Calu Wetuna, Painetuna and Uluerestuna)
Wihtric	free man (patron Harold, Scoteleia)

Majority OE. A significant number Scandinavian, or anglicised Scandinavian. A few ContGerman i.e. Robert, possibly Osbern, Fridebern and Strangwulf. Wymarc Breton

Personal-names of Scandinavian origin or flavour were recorded in most of the vills:

Alfildestuna
Alwartuna
Calu Wetuna
Cherchetuna
Herchesteda
Painetuna
Scoteleia
Stottuna
Torp
Turchetlestuna
Uluerestuna
Wervesteda

None recorded in
Beria
Eure Wardestuna
Holebroc
Torintuna, where all were OE

54 The site of St Clement's Chapel in Harkstead parish seen from the air in 1979. It is increasingly in danger of collapse onto the Stour foreshore as continuing erosion attacks the cliff on which the site stands. (Photograph I. MacMaster)

No pattern can be deduced from this distribution. It may be significant that personal-names showing long-term influence of Scandinavian origins were still in use in almost all the peninsula vills in 1066.

Danish influence in surnames

Thurketil's name persisted (in various spellings) in Shotley place-names into the eighteenth century, and is still the source of surnames today — 19 Thurkettles are listed in the current (2000) edition of the Ipswich area telephone directory. ON Ketill (in Ketylscroft in Woolverstone 1502) has also proved exceptionally long-lasting as a surname — 12 Kettles are now living in the Ipswich area. The Woolverstone name may have been derived from the Danish personal-name Ketill that became popular in England or it may have arisen as a nickname for a round-headed man with Danish forbears.[19]

Brand's name lived on in surnames (various spellings) widespread throughout the eastern half of the peninsula at least until the seventeenth century. The locative surname Fletesmewth, also recorded in various forms, was common in the peninsula's eastern coastal region. It probably evolved from a place-name derived from OE *fleot* 'estuary, inlet, creek' and OE *mutha* 'the mouth of a large river, an estuary' but the name may have been a hybrid containing ON *fljót* 'a river'.[20] It was a most appropriate name for people living in settlements grouped around the peninsula's numerous creeks and inlets.

St Clement's Chapel (**54**), Harkstead, was last recorded in a sixteenth-century will; its cemetery was named as a boundary later in the same century. OS maps mark the site close to the Stour shore. This dedication has Danish links and points to the trans-North Sea connections established after the conquest by Cnut (Barbara Crawford, pers. comm.).[21]

Danish influence in minor names

The documentary record yields some minor names that are clearly derived from Old Norse. For example, The Lounde in Erwarton from ON *lúndr*, for which there is no OE equivalent. In the Colton area of Shotley parish, Blaze Hill and Lower Blaze Field were listed in an 1827 deed.[22] The word Blaze may have been derived from the ON by-name Blesi[22] or from ON *blesi* 'bare spot on a horse's forehead', perhaps used topographically to indicate a bare spot on a hillside.[23] Ordnance Survey maps mark a triangulation point on the top of Blaze Hill. This nineteenth-century name suggests that the hilltop may have been the site of a fiery beacon — perhaps used to guide Viking ships in the Orwell or to warn of their presence. There is no evidence to support this suggestion; local fieldwork and further documentary research might be worthwhile.

In Woolverstone the ON word *hvin* 'gorse' is still remembered in the name Whinney Field Wood though the Whinny Field (1628) 'overgrown with gorse' now produces arable crops. Shotley Gate is the name of a modern housing development in Shotley parish. The Shotley Tithe Map (1839) marks two Shotley Gate Fields and Shotley Gate Meadow on either side of Bristol Hill (the road leading down to the riverside). Derivation from ON *gata* 'a way, a path a road'[24] is possible but unsafe without earlier spellings. The name may have referred to a gated farm road.

Harkstead's Wronge Oake (1568) 'the crooked oak' contains the ON adjective *vrangr*.[25]

11 Living in the Shotley Peninsula

Communications: trackways, bridges and fords

The Shotley Peninsula is almost entirely bounded by water: the tidal River Bourne and the eastern end of Belstead Brook separate it from the southern suburbs of Ipswich, the tidal estuaries of the Orwell and Stour define it to the east and south and on the west the lower ground is separated from neighbouring Brantham by the Samford River. The peninsula's central plateau rises westwards from less than 100ft to heathlands in Tattingstone and Belstead reaching c.150ft.

The area was heavily populated in prehistoric times. One of Suffolk's three Neolithic causewayed enclosures was in Freston. Clusters of ring ditches, no longer visible on the ground, mark the sites of numerous Bronze Age burials.[1]

Many of the trackways shown on air photographs originated in prehistoric times. Some, mostly on dry land above the spring line, remained in use in later periods, linking Romano-British settlements, and continuing long afterwards as the Common Ways described in manorial records. Others still exist as minor lanes, farm tracks and public footpaths. A long curving route linking the Orwell and Stour estuaries can be followed, using farm tracks and paths, all the way from Hill House in Shotley (in the site of Thurketelton) to Erwarton Creek. This may have marked an early boundary in Danish Kirkton cum Thorp.

Travellers in the Late Iron Age and Romano-British periods, living near tidal creeks, would have used waterways (**59**). If a low-lying track linking these sites once ringed the peninsula, continuing the line of Wherstead Strand, rising water levels and continuing erosion have submerged it.

In the Roman and later periods most settlements in the Shotley Peninsula were at or above the 50ft contour. Although streams were (and still are) numerous, generally they are narrow and unlikely to have been difficult to cross but fords were needed where important destinations could not be reached otherwise. Their sites are marked by the bridges that replaced them. In this way 15 fords have been traced, 12 wholly within the peninsula's parishes and three more connecting routes in the adjacent parishes: Bentley, Tattingstone and Brantham. They are listed below and their probable sites illustrated in (**55**).

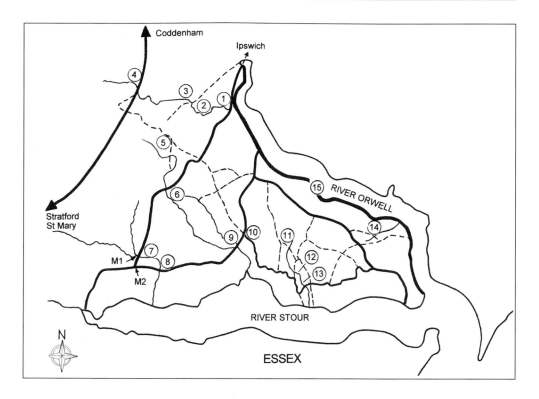

55 Fords and bridges in the peninsula

Bridges marking former fords in the Shotley Peninsula area

Fords F1-15 anticlockwise

F1	Bourne Bridge (Oreford)	TM 1620 4195
F2	Footbridge, Bobbits Hole (Hyford)	TM 1481 4148
F3	Belstead Bridge (Thief's Ford)	TM 1438 4192
F4	Honeyford Bridge (?Honeyford, where Roman road crossed Belstead Brook at Washbrook★)	TM 1099 4234
F5	Footbridge near Hubbards Hall (?name★★)	TM 1358 3950
F6	Bridge at Bentley Mill (Ford, name unknown)	TM 1340 3811
F7	Brantham Bridge (Saunford)	TM 1240 3511
F8	Stutton Bridge (Ford, name unknown)	TM 1350 3450
F9	Bridge at Alton Mill (?Ford, name unknown)	TM 1571 3582
F10	Bridge at Holbrook Mill (?Ford, name unknown)	TM 1695 3559
F11	Bridge (Ford on ancient way NW from Erwarton Creek, via Dench Wood to ?Belstead)	TM 1922 3576
F12	Bridge (Ford on route linking Stour and Orwell: Holbrook Bay to Pin Mill, Chelmondiston)	TM 1921 3510

56 Freston reach in the Orwell river — waterway to Europe. (Photograph J. King)

F13   Rat Bridge now, Ropkins Bridge 19c (?Godhelms Ford) TM 2041 3440
F14   'Charity Farm' Bridge (Ford, name unknown, on
      track linking Colton Creek and Hill House, Shotley)   TM 2302 3671
F15   Bridge lost (Sandy Ford, on riverside route through Chelmondiston
      Santon between Pin Mill and Woolverstone)   est. TM2032 3830

★Honeyford over the Wassebrok temp EdII (Copinger, Suffolk Records and MSS)
★★Name illegible in relevant deed (HD 210 1/53)

The earliest fords would have been associated with routes to the Samford Hundred Meeting Place. Originally this was at a sandy ford — long since replaced by Brantham Bridge on A137 (TM 1240 3524) — where two streams meet to form the Samford River. Later (date unknown) this open air meeting place was abandoned in favour of a hilltop site marked Saunford White House on Bryant's 1826 map of Suffolk.[2] Earlier names for this house were Saunfords and Stamfords; Brantham Court Farm now occupies the site at the top of Brantham Hill (Ruth Keeble, *Brantham Hall*, pers comm). The Hundred — nominally a hundred hides *c.*120a — was the basic unit of local administration at least from the tenth century, and earlier in some instances, as here. Business was dealt with at courts that met regularly at a specific place — the Moot Stow: OE *(ge)mōt* 'an assembly or meeting' with OE *stow* 'a place'.[3]

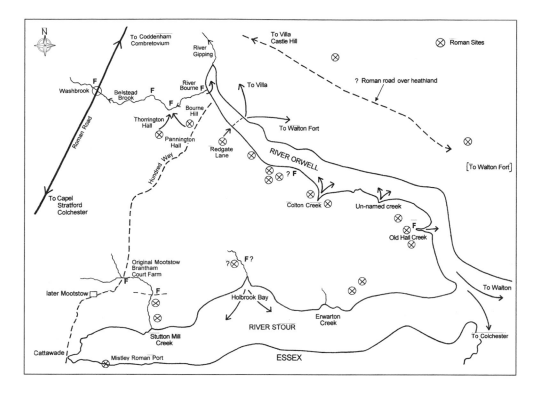

57 *Trade-routes in and beyond the peninsula in the Roman period in relation to known Roman sites and major Roman roads*

The main route to the Samford Hundred Meeting Place from settlements in the north east of the peninsula was The Hundred Way.[4] It started from Bourne Hill (Wherstead) and continued over heathland to the top of Brantham Hill, fording the Holbrook stream and the Samford River en route. It appears to correspond with the route of A137 before this road was diverted round Alton Water Reservoir. The ford (F5) was bridged (date unknown) near the site of Bentley Mill in Tattingstone; both were lost under the reservoir. The Saunford (F6) was replaced at an unknown date by Brantham Bridge on A137.

The main route to the Hundred meeting-place from settlements in the south east of the peninsula required a ford (F8) over the Samford River in Stutton. The bridge that replaced it was in existence in the thirteenth century when the adjacent Breggewode was the subject of dissention between the Prior and Canons of Dodnash Priory and Sir William Visdelou, then lord of Stutton Manor.[5]

Both routes out of the peninsula converged at the hilltop meeting place with routes from the north and west of Samford Hundred.

Two important fords allowed access from the peninsula to Gipeswic. Oreford (F1) — 'the ford by the shore' — connected the network of ways from within the peninsula that met at the bottom of Bourne Hill with a riverside way leading directly into the south of Gipeswic. Wherstead Road and Great Whip Street preserved this line of approach until recent development drastically altered the street layout. The exact site of Oreford is not known, nor is the date of the bridge that replaced it. In 1312 Robert de Reymes, lord of Wherstead Manor, left '20s for building (? repairing) the bridge at B…' in his will.[6] Unfortunately, the rest of the name is illegible but it seems reasonable to assume that it bridged the River Bourne. No record of when the Bourne was first bridged has been found. Modern Bourne Bridge, opened in 1983, bypassed a seventeenth-century seven-arched brick bridge still in place but no longer used

Theofford — The Thief's Ford (F3) — probably began as a link between local communities on either side of Belstead Brook in the Wherstead/Belstead area. It provided an alternative route from the peninsula to Gipeswic by the way that eventually became Belstead Lane, entering Gipeswic over a bridge at Stoke. Belstead Bridge marks the site of the ford. Cyril Hart's derivation of its name is supported by numerous references to Theford (various spellings) as a local surname in thirteenth-century Wherstead records.[7]

Hyford (F2) at Bobbits Hole was named in a sixteenth-century will.[8] It probably marked the site of an earlier ford giving access to water mills in this area, including two on the south side of the estate of Stoke (by Ipswich) granted by King Edgar to Ely Abbey in 970.[9]

Other water mills reached by fords and bridges include F6 (Bentley Mill); F9 (Alton Mill) and F10 (Holbrook Mill). Dates of the earliest mills at these places are not known.

F13, ?Godhelms Ford, remembered in the Erwarton surname Godelesford (1380),[10] provided access to Harkstead's medieval mill near Beaumont Hall and also to Erwarton Creek, from settlements on the east side of the stream. Ancient long-distance ways across the central peninsula required fords at FF11 and 12, marked now by bridges on minor roads. The ford (F14), now bridged, west of Charity Farm, Shotley, linked settlements at Colton Creek, dating from the Late Iron Age and the Romano-British period, with others in the vicinity of present-day Hill House Farm. This route is still in use as a farm track.

F15, the sandy ford remembered in an eighteenth-century field-name, served a route — now lost — between Chelmondiston and Woolverstone, then close to the Orwell shore.

Boats

The recurring theme of journeys by water and the evident importance of the peninsula's tidal rivers and creeks imply the widespread use of boats. Despite an

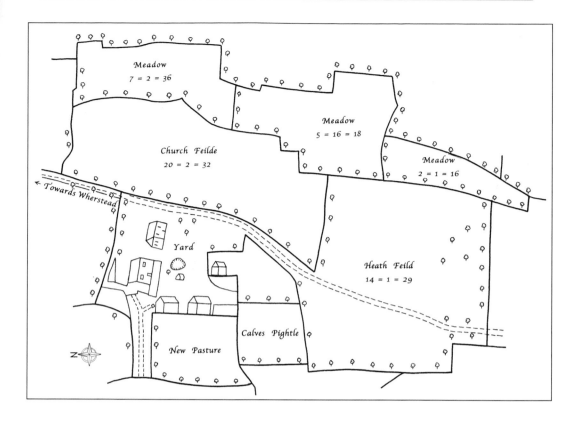

58 *The yards, fields and meadows of Thorington Hall (Wherstead) in 1676. A minster church occupied this land before the Norman Conquest. (Extract drawn from a 1676 plan of the estate in SROI)*

extensive literature on boat design and boat building in general, virtually nothing is known about the boats used as local transport by East Anglia's inhabitants during the first millennium AD and there are no specific records of boats used for more distant journeys.[11]

A few boat relics have been found in waters around the Shotley Peninsula. A 'log boat' discovered on the Stour shore at Harkstead in the 1920s is believed to be in the Fitzwilliam Museum, Cambridge. In 1996 an aerial photograph revealed timbers that appeared to be the remains of a boat, lying on inter-tidal mudflats in Holbrook Bay at Shallager Creek (STU 033 TM 1713 3278). They have not yet been examined.

In 1910 dredgers recovered parts of an oak dugout boat from the Orwell 'opposite Pond Ouze Point', Nacton. The findspot is recorded as TM 17..40.. (IPS Misc 10593). They may have been parts of the 'dugout canoe' dredged from the Orwell in Freston Reach (**56**), but not retained (FRT 004 TM 191398). Saxo-Norman pottery sherds found on the mudflats off Shotley Point probably came from a wreck but no boat remains have been found in the vicinity. Inter-tidal survey of the Orwell and Stour estuaries may add to this meagre record.

Spheres and influence: economic and political

In the last years of the Iron Age the Shotley Peninsula lay in the centre of Trinovantian territory as part of Cunobelin's kingdom. His coinage, minted in Colchester, was used by traders in Europe as well as locally. The discovery of Cunobelin coinage in the peninsula poses questions about trade connections impossible to answer until more coins are found.

In the Roman period numerous settlement sites overlooked the Orwell and Stour estuaries. Recovered coins and fragments of imported pottery and amphorae indicate wealth derived from surplus output available for trading after tax demands had been met. Some goods would have been exchanged locally. Since most — perhaps all — of these Romano- British settlements were close to streams or tidal creeks flowing into the estuaries, markets beyond the peninsula would have been readily accessible by water, using shallow-draft boats or sea-going craft. Other inland markets would have been reachable on foot or by horse and cart.

Some possible external trading routes are listed and illustrated in **57**.

Roman period trade routes out of the Shotley Peninsula

1. To the Roman road from Colchester to Coddenham (Combretovium) via Belstead Brook, meeting this road at Washbrook.
2. Overland to meet this Roman road at Lattinford and from there to the settlement (?villa) at Windmill Hill, Capel.
3. Via the Rivers Orwell and Gipping to Coddenham.
4a. To the Walton (Felixstowe) Roman settlement and later Roman fort, by sea from the Orwell and Stour estuaries and perhaps
4b. overland via a causeway at Redgate Hard.
5. To Colchester via the Roman road from a harbour or port on the south side of the Stour estuary at Mistley, Essex.
6. To Colchester's early port at Fingringhoe by sea from the Orwell and Stour estuaries.

Shops and markets in Colchester city would have been within reach. A Roman road, linking Colchester with a port on the Stour estuary at Mistley (North Essex), could have provided a trade route for settlements on the Suffolk side of the Stour. Droughts in 1976 revealed *c*.10km of a route linking Colchester with

Mistley on the river Stour.[12] The early Romano-British settlement and, later, the harbour and shore fort at Walton (Felixstowe) in operation in the third and fourth centuries, would have provided additional trading opportunities.

One market may have been provided by the Roman villa complex at Castle Hill, Ipswich, which dates from the second-century AD.[13] Finds from excavations in the 1930s and 1948-50 indicate considerable wealth and possibly industrial activity. In the third and fourth centuries AD, the harbour and shore fort at Walton (Felixstowe) would have provided additional trading opportunities.

On present evidence the Shotley Peninsula seems to have been bypassed by migrants, perhaps remaining a self-contained enclave of Romano-British influence into the fifth century, centred on Colchester (John Newman, pers comm). Its relationship with the emergent kingdom of East Anglia centred at Rendlesham in the Deben Valley is not known. Economic activity in the peninsula in the Middle Saxon period, influenced by activities in Gipeswic, may have included development at the Redgate Hard at Wherstead and at a trading centre associated with the Santon/Overton settlements. Danish occupation in the late ninth century and recurrent Viking attacks on Gipeswic (Ipswich) in the tenth/eleventh centuries diminished the town's importance in international trade but local trade continued.

Danish influence in the south-east of the peninsula, attested by the place-names Kirkton and Thorpe, has been discussed in chapter 10. The occurrence of the place-names Kirkby le Soken and Thorpe le Soken in north-east Essex suggests that these resulted from Danish settlement dating from the same period. Whether there were any connections between the two groups is an open question. The possibility that there was a hitherto unknown Danish fortification on the Suffolk side of the Stour suggests that a cross-Stour link between Danish army groups may have existed, briefly, in the early eleventh century. Harwich, on the north-east Essex coast, was Herewic, 'army camp' in 1248: Mills adds 'probably that of a Viking army'. Current place-name research in Essex and further investigation in Suffolk in the vicinity of Erwarton Creek may throw new light on the Danish history of the region.

A different, peaceful connection between north-east Essex and south-east Suffolk is recorded in the Domesday Survey: Harold held land in Harkstead as an outlier of his Essex manor at Brightlingsea.[14]

Religious influences: Pagan and Christian

Christian practice, never widespread in Britain during the Roman period, was revived in the years following Augustine's mission to convert the heathen population. From 600 the Roman Church gained adherents in the English

103

kingdoms, its influence spreading 'from the top down' as individual kings and their followers accepted the Christian faith, but in rural areas heathen habits lingered. Local sites in the peninsula associated with heathenism, identifiable by place-names, can be traced in eight of the nine parishes: closer study would surely reveal more.

Woodland shrines

The commonest pointer is the word harrow, derived from the OE(Angl) word *haerg*, meaning a heathen temple or shrine, or a sacred grove.[15] Places called The Harrow in Freston and Woolverstone were associated with ancient woodland.

In Freston The Harrow was the name of a small wood enclosed within its own banks, standing on high ground above Freston Brook close to the parish boundary with Wherstead. It belonged to Bond Hall manor. Recently it was taken into the Paul Estate's Stalls Valley Wood.[16]

Le Harrow in Woolverstone was in or near Dench Wood — 'the wood of a Saxon man called Denic'. This ancient bluebell wood, probably the 'wood for 16 pigs' recorded in the Domesday Survey, remains now as a small area of derelict trees surrounded by arable land in which the site of the pagan shrine has been lost.[17]

The Chelmondiston Tithe Map includes a field called The Harrow on high land above Pin Mill Lane. This name probably referred to the harrow-like shape of the field. An earlier reference to Le Harrow 'on land lately built' is more likely to point to a former pagan shrine. This land, Ashtree Field, was known as Tom Pooley's Piece in the eighteenth century and named Old Toms on the 1839 Tithe Map, which locates it next to the Chelmondiston/ Woolverstone parish boundary where Berners Lane met the Common Way (**43**). An indenture conveying two acres in Chelmondiston from Thomas Clapp and William Lemminge to Tom Pooley, and other related documents, are held in the Suffolk Record Office.[18]

Another Harrow, recorded from 1594 to 1823, was in the hamlet of Colton which belonged to Kirkton manor in Shotley parish. Its site has not been discovered. No early references to woodland associated with this place have been found.

The Lounde in Erwarton, named in 1594, derived its name from the Old Norse word *lúndr*, meaning a sacred grove, one offering sanctuary.[19] Whether the Danes adopted an existing Saxon haerg or chose their own grove is not clear. The site is not known.

The site of The Harrow in Harkstead, named in 1735 in a list of manor lands, is also unknown.[20]

When Holbrook records are searched they may reveal indications of pagan worship in the woods of Holbrook Park.

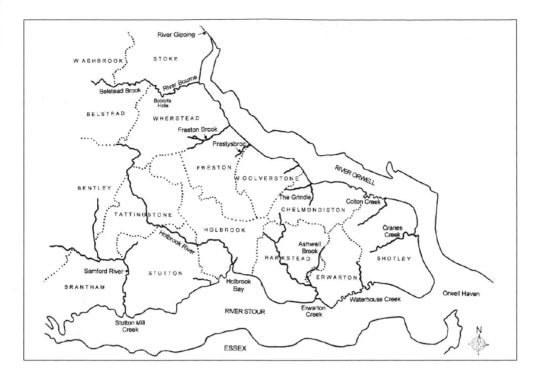

59 The peninsula's waterways and parish boundaries

Holy wells and sacred springs

Springs and wells, vitally important as sources of water, were venerated as the homes of capricious water gods and goddesses, to be propitiated by offerings thrown into the water. Holywell Meadow and Helwell Hill were in Freston manor land, later Freston Park.[21] These names are derived from the Old English word *hael* 'omen, good fortune'[22], so the Holy Well probably survived for a time as a wishing well.

In Erwarton, the spring marked Holy Well on a 1770 map fed a large lake in the grounds of Erwarton Hall.[23] In the eighteenth century this lake provided Harwich with drinking water when the shallow wells there were brackish. Supplies were delivered by boat from a quay in Waterhouse Creek.[24] All the water required by the Naval shore station HMS Ganges (in Shotley) in the early 1900s was pumped from the Erwarton Lake (Ted Mower, Shotley, pers comm). Such a copious spring would have attracted many 'well-wishers' in the past but any remnants of things thrown into the water lie in the depths of the lake, now a farm reservoir.

Other pagan religious sites

Swineshead, nineteenth-century glebeland in Shotley, recorded as Swenyhed in a 1380 Kirkton rental in place of the crossed-out word Belished/?Belsted, may suggest the existence of a primitive cult centre, perhaps devoted to a form of devil worship involving a pig's head mounted on a pole.[25] Dickens,[26] in EPNS XI (Surrey), discusses Bradley's suggestion that some animal-head field-names containing the element -heafod 'a head' may relate to heathen sacrifice. An alternative suggestion, that such names may refer to the shape of the field, does not fit in Shotley where the field — shown on the 1838 Tithe Map — appears sharply angular. With so little evidence available the existence of this form of devil-worship in Shotley parish seems beyond proof.

In Harkstead parish a site associated with the heathen god Woden seems more likely, but it has yet to be recognised.

The Churches

Nothing is known about the foundation of the peninsula's first churches, nor about the design and construction of the earliest buildings. The extent of the changes made in the post-Domesday centuries is made clear in the excellent guide books provided in all the parish churches but only archaeological survey can chart their earliest histories.

Church Sites

Pope Gregory advised Augustine to encourage church-building on pagan sites. The men who shared the cost of building St Peter's church in Stutton may have followed his advice. A spring in the churchyard feeds a stream that flows into the Stour via Markwell's Farm. Perhaps it was once venerated as the home of a water god or goddess.

Harkstead church — St Mary's — may have been sited to counter the influence of Woden, whose by-name Grim could have been the source of the Harkstead field-name Grimesdon. Its founder may have been the Saxon called Hereca or the Dane called Brand.

Wherstead church, also dedicated to St Mary, stands isolated between the village (Wherstead Street) and Wherstead Old Hall, on a level platform within a rectangular churchyard; there is a near-vertical drop on the eastern boundary. The church site appears to have been part of the western embankment of a very large rectangular enclosure of unknown date, no longer visible except in aerial photographs (**8**). Whether this enclosure influenced the founder's choice of the church site is not known; the significance of the site is not yet clear.

St Peter's, Freston, also isolated, stands at the corner of a lane that runs along the south boundary of Freston Wood. Very large oak trees mark the churchyard boundary. There is no evidence that this was a pagan site but the close proximity of Freston's ancient woodland may be significant.

Shotley church, dedicated to St Mary, is near Kirkton (Shotley) Manor Hall. This church would have belonged to the Saxon settlement re-named Kirkton by the Danes who settled there in the ninth century. It stands on the edge of high ground that falls steeply to the south and east. Nothing is known about its early history.

Holbrook church, dedicated to All Saints, is in the village on a hill overlooking the Holbrook stream. It is said to be a post-Domesday foundation.

Two of the peninsula's churches, both close to former manor halls, may have been founded by Saxon estate holders: Woolverstone's, dedicated to St Michael the Archangel, by Wulfhere and Chelmondiston's, dedicated to St Andrew, by Ceolmund. The founder of St Mary's in Erwarton may have been *Eoforweard. Most of the peninsula's churches were not recorded in the Domesday Survey; Painetuna's church with three acres has disappeared.

Minster or monastery?

The church with 50 acres in Torintuna (DB 11 f.426a) was probably a minster founded in the eleventh century by Stigand, whose free man Alwin held the jurisdiction of the manor of Torintuna in 1066.[27] Stigand was a royal priest; he was Bishop of Elmham, East Anglia in 1043, and Bishop of Winchester and Archbishop of Canterbury in 1053 until deposed in 1070.[28]

The church in Torintuna left no traces but the history of its 50 acres can be followed through field-names associated with lands that later belonged to the manor of Thorington. The plan held in the Suffolk Record Office depicting the lands and yards of Thorington Hall in 1676 shows Church Feilde (20 acres) immediately north-east of the Hall buildings, adjacent to three meadows (20 acres) and Heath Feilde 'now called Stony Downe' (14 acres) (**58**).[29] Together they formed a block with a total area of 54 acres. In later years Church Field dwindled in size. In 1847 the Great Eastern Railway line cut through it and the land south-west of the railway was annexed to Pannington Hall but Thorington Hall Farm still included a 14-acre Church Field in the late 1960s.[30]

The idea that 'a monastery' existed in Wherstead rests on the evidence of two deeds of the twelfth and thirteenth centuries. For a fine of 14s Gerard de Penitun (Pannington in Wherstead parish) granted land to William son of Edmund. This undated deed is believed to be of twelfth-century origin.[31] It refers to land in Perecroft and the adjacent marsh where the mill stands and land which Ediva held

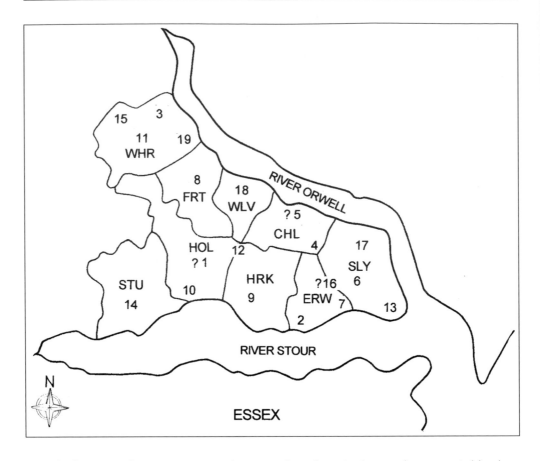

60 *The locations of DB manors now known to have been in the area later occupied by the Shotley Peninsula's nine parishes*

'infra monasterium de Wervesteda'. A fine dated 1190 confirms that William, Prior of St Peter, Ipswich, acquired land in Paninton Pannington).[32]

Stowe Charter 410 dated 'temp HenIII' (ie 1216-72) describes the same land as that detailed in the earlier deed and states that Gilbert, Prior of St Peter, granted it to Gilbert son of Robert de Reymes.[33]

In 1358 a piece of meadow, five other pieces of land and one cottage were granted to Robert Gore, his wife Petronella and son John.[34] The names of these fields — Pretelotleghe and Chapelmedwe — suggest that they had been part of the minster's territory.

Whether a 'monastery' or a second minster once existed in Wherstead parish in Pannington territory remains debatable. The Suffolk Record Society's forthcoming translation of the Priory's cartulary may clarify the problem. OE *mynster* 'a minster church with a community of secular priests', Latin *monasterium*, may mean either a minster, or a monastery in the generally accepted sense.

Hugh de Reymes built a chantry 'within his oratory within his Court of Querstede' in 1282.[35] If this oratory had been served by a monk it may have been seen — mistakenly — as a monastery. There is no basis for the idea that the elusive 'Wherstead monastery' was near Wherstead parish church (WHR Misc. 04709).

Parish boundaries

The laymen who built the first rural churches gained financially from the taxes and tithes they were able to levy. When these churches were removed from secular control, boundaries were needed to define parishes and so regulate church finances, but it was not until the early twelfth century that the boundaries were finalised. Streams and creeks flowing into the estuaries were used to define the lower reaches of the peninsula parishes; on the higher land the upper boundaries followed a line along the watershed (**59**). This arrangement cut through early settlements all over the peninsula. Most of the land belonging to Domesday Calu Wetuna (Colton) became part of Shotley parish but a small area on the west of Colton Creek is part of Chelmondiston parish. Chelmondiston and Woolverstone were separate parishes but treated as one unit in the 1387 subsidy tax returns, thus acknowledging the existence of Santon and Overton in the area between them. The ambiguity of the Erwarton/Harkstead parish boundary in the neighbourhood of Erwarton Creek has already been discussed. At higher levels, parish boundaries drawn across common heathland where there were no natural boundaries were somewhat vague. It was still possible in 1750 to refer to a Wherstead Hall tenement as 'Freston Heath in Wherstead'.[36]

12 The Shotley Peninsula in 1066

Besides its value as the source of almost all the peninsula's earliest place-names the Suffolk volume of the Little Domesday Book provides the first available information about the individual manors and lesser holdings in existence in 1066. With minor exceptions the Survey includes details of agricultural and industrial assets, working populations and the names of the people who held the land immediately before the Norman Conquest. For most of those described as free men the names of their patrons are also included.

The names of the peninsula's 30 individual holdings and their DB folio references are listed on p112; their industrial assets, including sheep for wool production and pigs as a measure of woodland, are analysed on p113. Basic agricultural assets — land and ploughs available for arable cultivation, meadows for hay, and various types of farm livestock — were too diverse to tabulate.

Clearly the peninsula was predominantly arable farmland. Even the smallest holdings with less than 100 acres had one or 'half' a plough. There were 18 ploughs on Herchesteda's two large manors; Fresetuna had ten. Presumably in a good year a surplus of grain would have been available for sale outside the peninsula but it is impossible to estimate the value of this essentially variable asset. Areas of arable land were recorded as carucates (*c.*120 acres). Most manors had one, one-and-a-half or two caruates; there were seven carucates in Herchesteda (Edeva's holding) and six in land held by Robert son of Wymarc in Fresetuna. Lesser holdings, recorded as acres in units from 5 to 100, totalled 19; most were 30 or 60 acres. How they were farmed is not stated.

Meadowland was relatively scarce; eight holdings had none and most had fewer than five acres. Painetuna had ten acres and the four manors named Stuttuna (in various spellings) together had eleven. The hay produced would have been used on the farms. Woodland was described in the Survey in terms of the number of pigs that could be fattened on fallen acorns or beech mast in the autumn before being slaughtered, salted and stored for winter. This was a conventional measure used in the eastern counties to indicate the size of a wood.[1] Only three woods in the peninsula were recorded in this way: Herchesteda (30 pigs), Stotuna (16 pigs), and Uluerestuna (15 pigs). No other data for woodland were given though ancient woodland, known to have existed in the peninsula in

Holbrook Park, Freston Wood and Cutlers Wood, would have been valuable sources of timber and coppice wood.[2]

Many of the lesser holdings had no livestock and in general the numbers of cattle, sheep, goats, farm pigs and horses were small; there were two oxen.

Despite the omission of Chelmundestun and incomplete assessment of woodland assets, it is clear that the peninsula's manors were notably rich. On the Orwell side the values recorded for the four holdings in Wherstead parish — Wervesteda, Painetuna, Torintuna and Beria — totalled £9; Fresetuna was valued at £8. The contribution of Ceolmundestun, included in the assessment for Hintelsham, has been estimated as £12 (p79). When Turchetlestuna (£2) and Calu Wetuna (5s 4d) are included the total value of the Orwell-facing manors comes to £31 5s 4d.

On the Stour side Herchesteda's two large manors, valued together at £16, were the richest in the peninsula. Alwartuna and Eurewardestuna were valued (in error) at £2 and 8s respectively; the figures should be 8s and £2 respectively. Holebroc's single holding was valued at £1. The four holdings in Stuttona — two large manors and two lesser ones — were worth a total of £8 10s, bringing the value of the Stourside holdings to £29 10s. At the tip of the peninsula Scoteleia was valued at £9. Possession of mills, salthouses, fisheries and beehives accounts for much of this wealth; grain and wool would have produced additional earnings not recorded. The total value of the Shotley Peninsula holdings is estimated as *c.*£70.

In 1066 almost every manor and lesser holding in the peninsula was held by Harold, his brother Earl Gyrth, his mistress Edeva, or their thegns and free men. Harold held the territorial jurisdiction of East Anglia and north Essex *c.*1045 and on the eve of the Norman Conquest Earl Gyrth's lesser jurisdiction included both Suffolk and Norfolk.[3] Edeva, Ediva, 'the Fair', 'the Rich' was Edith Swan-Neck, first wife of Harold Godwineson, King Harold II. This marriage was not recognised by the Church. In 1066 she held lands, mostly in eastern England, worth more than £520.[4]

The evident prosperity of the Shotley Peninsula's Domesday communities was based, fundamentally, on the natural assets of the area which had been exploited — often with marked success — by earlier groups of people. Although there is no written record of their history, archaeology, combined with place-name research, has begun to suggest where people lived and how and why their fortunes varied throughout the first millennium AD. Present understanding, though limited, is enough to show where further research is likely to be most productive. Meanwhile the evidence presented here summarises the situation as it was in 1066 (**60**).

The Felixstowe peninsula, comprising the Hundred of Colneis, lies between the tidal estuaries of the Orwell and Deben, with its south-east coast exposed to the North Sea. Though its geology and soils resemble those of the Shotley Peninsula, its historical development through the first millennium AD and its markedly different topography differentiate it from its neighbour. How these differences affected developments in the two peninsulas have yet to be investigated.

The Shotley Peninsula's Domesday place-names

*Alfildestuna	ff 378a, 420a
Alwartuna	f 394b
*Beria	f 295a
Calu Wetuna	f 295b
*Canapetuna	f 296a
*Canepetuna	f 418b
Cherchetuna	f 395a
(Kirkton)	
Eure Wardestuna	f 395a
Fresetuna	f 395b
Frisetuna	f 402a
Herchesteda	ff 286b, 420b, 430b
Holebroc	f 295a
Painetuna	ff 295b, 402a
*Purte pyt	f 394b
Scoteleia	ff 287a, 394b
**Scottuna	f 411b
Stotuna	f 419b
Stottuna	f 296a
Stuttuna	f 420a
Torintuna	f 426a
*Torp	f 394b
*Turchetlestuna	f 420a
Uluerestuna	f 295b
Hulferestuna	f 420a
Weruesta	f 402a
Wervesteda	f 295b

*unidentified in Domesday Gazetteer, Darby and Versey, Cambridge 1975, but traced in the peninsula
**presumed Stuttuna

Assets of the Shotley Peninsula's DB manors 1066

	Assets	Population*
Orwell-side		
Beria (Bourne)	1 mill	5
Painetuna	1 salthouse 80 sheep	35
Torintuna	1 mill	60
Wervesteda	1 salthouse	30
Fresetuna	1 mill, wood (40 pigs)	165
Uluerestuna	Wood (15 pigs)	40
?Chelmundestun	?1 salthouse ?1 mill	?5
Calu Wetuna		5
Turchetlestuna	2/3 fishery	20
Cherchetuna (Kirkton)		25
		total *c*.390
Peninsula tip		
Scoteleia		total 135
Stour-side		
Alwartuna	1/3 fishpond	65
Torp		20
Herchesteda	1 mill, wood (30 pigs)	345
Purte pyt		35
Holebroc		5
Scottuna	1 salthouse 2 beehives	70
Stotuna	2 salthouses 1 mill	100
Stottuna		15
Stuttuna		5
Alfildestuna	1 mill	5
		total *c*.665

*Working population estimated as five times the numbers of villagers, smallholders, slaves and free men.

Totals must be regarded as very approximate. The figures suggest that the peninsula's working population in 1066 was probably of the order of 1000. Total value estimated: £70.

The Felixstowe peninsula's Domesday place-names

Alteinestuna	ff 292a, 341a, 341b, 342b
★Brihtolevestuna	f 406a
Bukelesha, Buclesha	ff 292a, 386b
Buregata	f 339b
Burch, Burg	ff 340a, 423b
Candelenta	f 341a
★Carlewuda	f 314b
Faltenha	ff 339b, 340b, 423b/424a
Grimestuna	ff 292a, 341b
Gulpelea	f 340a
Guthestuna	f 340b
Helmelea, Halmeleia, Halmelega, Helmelea, Helmele	ff 340b, 349b, 424a, 431a, 431b
★Hopewella	f 314b
★Iste uerestona (sic)	f 406a
Kenebroc, Kinebroh, Kenebroc, Kelebroc	ff 340b, 343a, 385b, 441b
Kirketuna	ff 340b, 342b, 423b
★Kul- Kyluertestuna, ★Culuerdestuna	ff 342b, 406a
Langestuna	ff 341b, 341b
Leofstanestuna	ff 342a, 342a/b
Leuetuna	ff 341a
Maistana	f 339b/340b
Morestuna; Morestona; Mothestuna	ff 292a, 385b; 423b; 340b, 342b
Morestona	f 424a
Mycelgata	ff 314b, 342a
Nachetuna	f 406a
Nortuna	ff 340a, 342a

Oxelanda	f 343a
Plumgeard	f 340a/b, 385b
Strattuna	ff 314a/b, 342b/343a
★Struustuna: ★Struestuna	ff 340b, 341b, 341b
Torp, Torpa	ff 292a, 342b, 341b
Tre'lega, Tremlega, Tremelaia	ff 385b, 342b, 423b
Wadgata	ff 340a, 342a
Waletuna	ff 339b, 385b, 406b

★'unidentified'

★Carlewuda, ★Hopewella and ★Kul- Kyluerestuna where free men, added to Strattuna 'after 1066', had been living

The Felixstowe peninsula's assets in 1066

Vills★   27 identified plus 5 not yet identified

Individual holdings   74

Arable land

      as carucates   in 10 vills, range from 1 or 2 carucates

      as acres   in all holdings, except 7, range 2 to 100a

           many 10 acres or less, smallest a half acre

Ploughs   total 84

      in all except 9 individual holdings

        several had half a plough

Meadows in all except 2 vills

      maximum 30a majority 1-2a

Assets   Mills: 5.2 in Kelebroc/Kenebroc

       1 each in Nachestuna, Leofstanestuna and

       Strattestuna

      Salthouses: 1 in Leofstanestuna

      Beehives: 0

      Woodland: Nachestuna (8 pigs)

       Strattuna (6 pigs)

      Fishery: 1 in Waletuna

      Sheep: rarely recorded

       140 in Waletuna 80 in Strattuna

      Other livestock: very few recorded

Working population   free men (women) 380 (3)

                                         Villagers 13

                                         smallholders 95

                                         total est *c.*500

Values		
	Waletuna and outlier Faltenham	£6 15s 0d
	Isteuerestuna	£4 10s 0d
	Strattuna	£4 4s 5d
	Nachestuna	£3 10s 0d
	Bukelesha'	£3 0s 0d
	Burch	£2 3s 0d
	Struestuna, Struuestuna	£2 3s 0d
	vills valued £2 or less (total)	£17 7s 4d
	Total value, round figures	£35

*vill — unit of assessment for tax

working population estimated as five times the numbers of free men and women, villages and smallholders: *c.*2,500.

Though the Felixstowe peninsula's estimated population, with its large numbers of free men, was much greater than that of the Shotley Peninsula, its value was only half the figure estimated for the latter.

13 A post-Domesday perspective

Rental of the Lord King for Saunford n.d. (?thirteenth century)

The township of Chelmondiston annual rent 100s 10d

The tenants of the manor of Erwarton annual rent 10s

The tenants of the major of Reydon (Raydon) annual rent 23s 10d

The tenants of the land late Nicholas Reymis annual rent 4s

The tenants of the land late Thomas Smyth of Reydon annual rent 14d

The tenants of the manor of Hygham (Higham) annual rent 6s

The tenement called Spanbys annual rent 11d

The tenants of the manor of Ouyrhalle (Overhall) annual rent (3s 4d struck out) 18d

The Prior of Legha (Leighs) for land in Wenham annual rent 3s 10d

The tenants of Churcheford in Capel annual rent 3s 8d

The tenement called Knebon annual rent 2d

The tenants of the manor of Wenham annual rent 3s 4d

The tenants of the manor of Vaus (Vaux) annual rent 11d

The tenants of the land called Brekelis annual rent 9d

The tenants of the land called Fastholfes annual rent 2s 5d

The Prior of Holy Trinity Ipswich annual rent 18d

The tenants of the manor of Stutton annual rent 7s

Helena Feudor annual rent 16d

The tenants of the manor of Boyton annual rent 2s 10d

The tenants of the manor of Braham (Braham Hall in Cattiwade in Brantyham) annual rent 4s

The tenant of the tenement called Lopham annual rent 11d

The tenant of lands late John Rery in Stutton annual rent 20s

The tenant of the tenement called Argentes annual rent 14d

The tenants of the manor of Holbrok for lands late William Brantham and Christina Sondirlond annual rent 2s 10d

William Rawmedewe annual rent 18s

The tenants of the manor of Kyrketon annual rent (5d struck through)

The tenants of the manor of Freston annual rent 3s 6d

The tenants of the manor of Kyrketon annual rent 22d

The tenants of Thinkekton annual rent 5d

The tenants of the manor of Wolferston annual rent 18d

The tenants of the manor of Bonds in Freston annual rent 3s 6d

The tenement called Brythmeris Fullere annual rent 22s

The tenement late of Roger Reymis annual rent 2s 8d

The Prior of St Peter, Ipswich, for Panygton annual rent 4s 10d

The tenants of the Lord King's land in Brustalle (Burstall) annual rent 3s 9d

The tenants of Brownis in Coppedoc annual rent 2s 1d

The tenants of the manor of Copdock annual rent 2s 1d

The tenants of the tenement of land in Dadyngston (Tattingstone) annual rent 2s 5d

The tenement and lands of Grotes in Capel annual rent 9d

The tenement and lands of John Accept annual rent 4d

Of William Brown annual rent 11d

The tenants of the manor of Sulleys in Reydon (Sulveyes or Sullies in Raydon) annual rent 6s

The tenants of the manor of (Stratton, struck through) Stratford annual rent 3s 8d.

Total £11 12s 1d

Account of ★fines of the lete of Saunford

The fine of Burmanberyelis annually 7s

The fine of Freston 14d

The fine of the church of Wersted (Wherstead) annually 3s

The fine of Werstead next to the church 12d

The fine of Dadyngston (Tattingstone) annually 2s

The fine of Braham (Brantham) in Stapilstrete annually 2s

The fine next to the church there annually 12d

The fine at Benteleyghe (Bentley) annually 12d

The fine at Capel 6d

The fine at Little Wenham annually 6d

The fine at Wenham Combust annually 3s 6d

The fine at Reydon annually 5s

The fine at Brustalle (Burstall) annually 18d

The fine of the manor of Braham annually 2s

The fine of the manor of Cherchefore (Churchford Hall in Capel St Mary) annually 6d

The fine of the manor of ?Anmarlehall (Amor Hall in Belstead) annually 2d

The fine of Stratford annually 7s

Total £2 0s 8d

★fine could also be farm, feorm 'rent in kind'

The dorse of the document is very badly faded; under ultra-violet light only the
    first ten entries legible
Dame Alice …
Dame Joan …
Augustine ?Stanton
Thomas Wolferson
The tenants of Wolferston Hall
Thomas St…of the same
Richard Legy of …
The tenants of the tenement Brythmersffullere
The Prior of St Peter Ipswich
Helena ?Brede
Joan Sondyrlond
Joan Brantham
The tenant of the tenement of the manor of Ovirhalle
The tenant of the tenement of Breklis
The tenant of the tenement of Knebonis
Gilbert Debyham
The tenant of Stutton Hall
Thomas Giffard with his fellows (sociis)
The tenant of the tenement of Barownis
The tenant of the tenement of Fastolfys
The tenant of Chercheford Hall
The tenant of the tenement Spanbys
The prior of Dodenasch
Richard Stratford

Source: HA 246/D/2 n.d. ?14c, SROI[1]
Translator: Marion Allen

14 Archaeological sites guide: Late Iron Age to 1066

Suffolk Archaeological Service: sites and monuments records

★ = metal detector find   Un = undated

Parish	Site	Period	Description
Late Iron Age (c.100 BC to AD 43)			
Chelmondiston			
CHL016	SF7345	IA★	Gold stater: Ambiani (Seaby No.1) 120-100 BC
CHL 017	SF8081	IA	Norfolk Wolf type stater, gold-plated bronze forgery
CHL 027	SF13704	IA★	Bronze coin, Trinovantian (Cunobelinus)
CHL 028	SF14278	IA★	Trinovantian gold stater British F type, wt 6.3g
Harkstead			
HRK 007	SF08312	Un?IA	Cropmarks show a roughly D-shaped enclosure with internal trackways, western entry, ditched tracks within
Holbrook			
HBK Misc	SF8158	IA	?Halstatt axe, found on construction site 15-20ft down
Shotley			
SLY 023	SF17996	IA★	2 LIA coins, dished bronze
SLY 031	SF711	IA★	Probable dispersed hoard of gold coins
SLY 036	SF712	IA★	Gold quarter stater Addedomaros (15-1 BC)
SLY 046	SF9116	IA★	Gold stater, Trinovantian British F type
SLY Misc	SF1758	IA★	Bronze coin, Dubnovellaunus

SLY Misc	SF8509	IA	Pottery, C1 type slight combing on shoulder

Stutton

STU 022	SF8292	IA	?Salt-making site and triangular loom weight exposed by tidal erosion beside River Stour

Wherstead

WHR 021	SF12739	IA	A few hand-made ?IA sherds from excavation of trackway flanking (E-W) ditches (cropmarks)
WHR 027	SF10926	IA	'A' sherds in pit and scatter outside excavated ring ditch
WHR 037	SF11605	IA	Enclosure ditches and other features excavated

Roman period

Arwarton

ARW 002	SF12490	Rom★	Frag. Colchester derivative brooch
ARW 014	SF9001	Rom★	Metalwork scatter N of cropmarks
ARW 031	SF16120	Rom★	?Rom padlock in bronze horse form

Chelmondiston

CHL 004	SF13249	Rom★	coin:worn ?late third-century *radiate*
CHL 010	SF10047	Rom★	Silver *denarius* Rom. Republican
CHL Misc	SF10048	Rom★	Finger ring, bronze, gold wash, crystal setting
CHL Misc	SF13549	Rom★	Frag. disc-type brooch
CHL Misc	SF7350	Rom★	Bronze belt stiffener
CHL Misc	SF9174	Rom★	Bronze coin (Ae2) of Magnentius (AD 350-351)

Freston

FRT 001	SF8551	Rom	Coin hoard mid C4 ploughed up

Holbrook

HBK 002	SF8148	Rom	Coin hoard C3-4
HBK 003	SF8149	Rom	Pottery: Samian & grey-ware sherds '6-8ft down'

Harkstead

HRK 013	SF8317	Rom	19 coins ploughed up over several years
HRK 019	SF12168	Rom★	Coin: *antoninianus* of Gallienus AD 253-60
HRK 032	SF9068	Rom★	*Denarius*, ?forgery silver plate on bronze core
HRK Misc	SF7353	Rom★	*Sestertius*, Trajan (AD 102-12)

Shotley

SLY 002	SF8466	Rom★	Coins, bronze, 3 of Constantine I (Trier)
SLY 006	SF12013	Rom★	Brooch, P-shaped type variant, enamelling traces
SLY 011	SF8475	Rom★	Coin C2
SLY 019	SF8484	Rom★	Coin, silver *denarius* of Aelius Caesar (AD 137)
SLY 023	SF17997	Rom★	Finds in undated cropmark area
SLY 031	SF8497	Rom★	Coins scatter
SLY 034	SF8501	Rom★	Coins, thin scatter
SLY 044	SF9453	Rom★	Silver *denarius* of Hadrian (AD 120-38)
SLY 048	SF12763	Rom★	Frag. Colchester derivative type brooch (rear hook)
SLY 052	SF12387	Rom★	Silver Republican *denarius* *c.*150 BC
SLY 053	SF12650	Rom★	3 coins: Antonius Pius (AD 138-61) — Commodus (AD 177-80)
SLY Misc	SF12169	Rom★	Frag. Colchester type brooch
SLY Misc	SF12388	Rom★	Parts of large bow brooch
SLY Misc	SF12395	Rom★	Illegible *denarius*
SLY Misc	SF14324	Rom★	Bronze coin, Ae3, AD 330-7
SLY Misc	SF14325	Rom★	Bronze coin, *as*, corroded, date unkown
SLY Misc	SF9171	Rom★	Bronze brooch frag. probably large Hod Hill type, much battered

Stutton

STU 014	SF6678	Rom★	8 *sestertii*, ?hoard, Stour Estuary beach
STU 023	SF9776	Rom	pottery 'Romano-British'
STU Misc	SF12017	Rom★	Trumpet brooch damaged
STU Misc	SF12018	Rom★	*Dupondius* of Claudius I irregular copy (*c.*AD 50-64)

Wherstead

WHR 001	SF4666	Rom	Coin hoard 9 in pot, AD 250-73
WHR 003	SF4668	Rom	Pottery sherds ?C1, found 1920 and *c.*1947
WHR 004	SF4669	Rom	Coin, Claudius Gothicus, with potsherds
WHR 009	SF4674	Rom	Potsherds, 1000+ on clay floor
WHR 010	SF4675	Rom	Potsherds dense scatter
WHR 011	SF4676	Rom	Frag. Neidermendig lava quern
WHR 012	SF4677	Rom	Pottery in extraction pit
WHR 013	SF4679	Rom	Coins found when digging house foundations
WHR 018	SF17516	Rom	9 potsherds in field-walking survey 60ha Pannington Hall B area
WHR 029	SF04695	?Un	Sub-rectangular enclosure (crop-marks)
WHR 030	SF7375	Rom★	Coin hoard scattered
WHR 036	SF7376	Rom★	Coins scatter Trajan (AD 98-117) — Constantinian (AD 335-41)
WHR 037	SF11606	Rom	2 double-flued pottery kilns overlying LIA enclosure
WHR 041	SF13390	Rom	Small pottery concentration Pannington Hall A area
WHR 050	SF17477	Rom★	10 Roman coins
WHR Misc	SF13394	Rom	Field-walking survey Pannington Hall, areas A and C
WHR Misc	SF4708	Rom★	Gold coin, ?date, in roadwork, village street to church
WHR Misc	SF7377	Rom	Blue glass bead melon-shaped type

Woolverstone

WLV 005	SF9384	Rom	'A few sherds of RB and Med. pottery accompanied the beaker pottery'
WLV 010	SF9389	Rom	Samian sherd on beach
WLV 015	SF7299	Rom★	Bronze brooch (Colchester deriv.) Mercury figurine Coins C1-4
WLV Misc	SF11767	Rom★	2 coins, Trajan (103-17) and Constans (337-50)
WLV Misc	SF11969	Rom★	Frag. bronze lock bolt with triangular perforations
WLV Misc	SF17733	Rom★	*Denarius*: Septimus Severus (AD 197)

Saxon period

Erwarton

ARW 023	SF11213	Sax★	Bronze strap-separator, 3 arms, conical centre

Chelmondiston

CHL 004	SF13250	Sax	Pottery sherds including 3 Thetford type rims
CHL 016	SF11392	Sax★	Cut half-penny of Aethelred II (978-1016) (quarter found)
CHL 031	SF16150	Sax★	Gilded bronze sword pommel with stylised ?animal heads
CHL Misc	SF10049	Sax★	Bronze strap-end fitting, decorated

Freston

FRT 007	SF11177	Sax	2-3 sherds Ipswich-ware in trench
FRT 022	SF1832	Sax★	Gold pendant C7 type, garnet and filigree
FRT 032	SF13432	Sax	Large sherd Ipswich-ware with rouletted decoration

Harkstead

HRK 028	SF9067	Sax★	Bronze quatrefoil strap-separator or belt fitting

Shotley

SLY 037	SF2272	Sax★	Bronze caterpillar brooch
SLY 047	SF10165	Sax★	Bronze plaque with beast decoration Ringerike style
SLY 050	SF11274	Sax★	Mid/Late Saxon belt mount, quadrilateral with 4 open sections near centre
SLY 053	SF13772	Sax★	Diamond-shaped stud/belt decoration four openwork panels in centre
SLY 056	SF13882	Sax★	Bronze brooch Urnes style, body of serpentine animal with interlaced tendrils

Stutton

STU 007	SF8233	Sax	2 Ipswich-ware pots from churchyard extension
STU 007	SF08295	Sax	Carved stone in church outer walls
STU 024	SF9777	Sax	Large rim sherd Ipswich-ware
STU 027	SF11221	Sax★	C9/C10 bronze strap-end fragment

STU Misc	SF8294	Sax	Four sherds Ipswich-ware, one stamped, on Stour foreshore

Wherstead

WHR 012	SF4678	Sax	'Pre-Norman' pottery C10/12
WHR 037	SF11607	Sax	One piece Ipswich-ware, 2 strap-ends
WHR 040	SF13391	Sax	1 base sherd ?Ipswich-ware Pannington Hall Area A

Woolverstone

WLV 012	SF14779	Sax	2 sherds Ipswich-ware, 5 Thetford-type ware in trench
WLV 017	SF11765	Sax★	Bronze disc brooch probably enamelled Maltese cross design C8-early C10 1 sceatt A series
WLV 019	SF12795	Sax★	Sceatt, Kentish series B type ?minted in London

15 Parish guide to Shotley Peninsula names

The place-names, field-names, personal-names and surnames discussed in this book are listed under parishes, presented in order round the peninsula from Wherstead to Stutton. This arrangement allows places on parish boundaries* to be related: early settlements, later divided when parish boundaries were fixed, are named in both parishes. Dates refer to the sources in which the names were found; they are not necessarily the earliest recorded.

* pre-1974 boundaries

Tidal Estuaries[1-3]

Orwell estuary Ar(e)wan 1016
Stour estuary   Sture/Stufe muthan 835
Orwell Haven   confluence of Orwell and Stour estuaries, current

Wherstead

Belstead Bridge, current
Belstead Brook, current, Wherstead/Ipswich boundary
Beria 1066
Blackamore Lands 1676, Blackmore Land 1838, Blacklands 1968
Bobbits Hole, current
Bone Hall 1700
Borne Hill Manor 1530
Bourne Hall Farm, current
Bourne Hall Farm House 1924/5, not now inhabited
Bowen Hall 1528
Bourne Bridge ?1312, present bridge 1983
Bourne Creek, Hill, Park, River, modern maps

Camp Yard, OS maps 1890, 1999
Church St Mary
Church Feilde 1676
Church Field 1968
Clamp Yard, brick works nineteenth/twentieth century, disused
Crabbe Lane alias Holbrook Lane 1700, both names lost
Donome Bredge 1538
Downham Bridge
?Dunna's Meadow (Dunhom) ?MidSax
Downham Reach in Orwell river, current
Freston Heath in Wherstead 1750
Gilbert, Prior of St Peter Ipswich
Gore, Robert 1358
Goreston, Robert de 1270
Hyford 1582
Knawebonwall/Knoubones Wall, Meadow, thirteenth century
Knobon, a tenement ?late thirteenth century
Lampets thirteenth century
Ordgar, Saxon personal-name
de Or(e)ford, surname thirteenth century
Osegorestun(e) strete ?late thirteenth century
Orgaston Street, 1399
Painetuna 1066
Painton late thirteenth century
Pannington Hall Manor, amalgamated with Thorrington Hall nineteenth century
Pannington Hall Farm, current
Panygton, late thirteenth century
Penitun 1216-1292
Perecroft ?thirteenth century
Pretelotleghe 1358
Querstede 1282
Redgate Farm, Hard, Hill, Lane, current
The Strand current
de Strond(e), le Stronde, surnames thirteenth century
The Strondweye, thirteenth century
Sparnis Walton, Sparr Walton, late thirteenth century
Stoney Downe 1676
de Theford, Thefford, Teford, Tetford surnames twelth/thirteenth century
Theofford 970, ford over Belstead Brook, Wherstead/Ipswich boundary
Thefford Bridge 1654, in perambulation of Ipswich Liberties 1352/3
Thor(r)ington Hall Farm, 1676 and current

Torintuna 1066
Werstead 'next to the church', tenement ?fourteenth century
Wersted, 'fine of the church of Wersted' ? fourteenth century
Wervesteda 1066
Wherstead Church St Mary ?n.d.
Wherstead Hall, current ('The Mansion')
Wherstead, parish name
Wherstead Old Hall, (medieval manor house, thirteenth century moated site)
Whersted Park, eighteenth-century mansion in the Park
Wherstead Street, current
Wherstead Vicarage and Lane nineteenth century

Freston

Aelflaed eleventh century
Bond Hall, current
Bonds Manor fourteenth century
Cutlers Wood
Fresentun *c.*1000, Fresetuna/Frisetuna 1066
Freston Brook, current
de Freston, surname thirteenth century
Freston Heath in Wherstead 1750
Freston Manor 1418
Freston, parish name
Freston Park, current
Freston Reach in the Orwell estuary, current
Freston Wood, ancient woodland, current
The Harrow (a wood) 1744, part of Stalls Valley Wood now
Helwell Hill, Holywell Meadow, 1640
Prestysbroc 1497, Freston/Woolverstone boundary
Stalls Valley Wood, current

Woolverstone

Brandeston (Bramston, Brampston), surname 1348, later elsewhere in the peninsula
Cafca, Saxon personal-name
Caketon 1348, 1419
The Cliff 1628, current

Common Way between Woolverstone and Chelmondiston n.d. ?Saxon
Crabbe Trees (an orchard) 1406
Curtelisdonlands (various spellings) 1635, 1672, 1774
Dench Wood, current
Densshwode 1348, Dennsshwood 1404, Dennysshwode 1524
Dontonstrete 1491
Dunton Walton 1460
Elbury Down 1683
Ketylscroft 1502, Kettlescroft 1686
Lopham (place-name) 1086-1749
Lopham, surname 1086
Lophams 1749
Lopymfeld 1348
Mannings Lane, current
Overton 1428
Purpette fifteenth century
Runtyngs 1488-1714
Santon 1419-sixteenth century?Woolverstone/Chelmondiston boundary
Uluerestuna, Hulferestuna 1066
Wolferston Manor Court 1348-1791
Wolverston, Elizabeth 1419
Wolverston, Richard 1419
Woolverstone church, St Michael and all Angels n.d.; reconsecrated St Michael
nineteenth century after reconstruction
Woolverstone Field 1830
Woolverstone Park Pale 1726
Woolverstone, parish name
Woolverstone Hall, Park, Street, Village, current
Woolverstone Old Hall eighteenth century

Chelmondiston

Affoswalle 1590
Apeltons 1599
Ashtree Field 18c
Berners Lane, current, Woolverstone/Chelmondiston parish boundary
Bramstons Lane 1490
Caketon 1419
Calu Wetuna 1066? Chelmondiston/Shotley
Ceolmund, Saxon personal-name

Ceolmundeston 1174
Chelendylondes 1521
Chelendlondes 1590
Chelmondiston Church Farm House
Chelmondiston Church, St Andrew, rebuilt and reconsecrated 1957
Chelmondiston Manor Hall 1316-1841
Chelmondiston Manor Farm, current
Chelmondiston Santon 1428
Chelmyngton *c.*1380
Estfeld (Common Field) 1590
The Grindle, stream
The Harrow 1654, 1839
Hollow Lane, current
Kaketon 1419
Kaketon, Blaise de, ?thirteenth century
Moweslowe Lane alias Bramstons Lane 1490
Old Toms 1839
Open Fields 1490
Overton 1428
Pages Common, current
Pin Mill, current
Richardsons Lane ,current
Runtyngs 1488, 1714
Salters 1599
Sandford, Great and Little, 1714
Santon 1419, Chelmondiston/Woolverstone boundary
Tom Pooleys Piece eighteenth century
Walton 1838
Wash Lane OS map 2_in/m 1955, Chelmondiston/Shotley boundary
Woolverstone Field 1726

Shotley

Alflyth *c.*1380
Belished/Belisted *c.*1380
Blaze Hill, Lower Blaze Field, 1827
Bristol Hill, current
Caketon fourteenth century
Caketon, Robert of Kyrketon 1410
Caketon, Robert 1449

Calton Field, 1594
Calu Wetuna 1066 Shotley/Chelmondiston boundary
Calverton 1776
Calverton Common 1790
Caluton c.1380, Shotley/Chelmondiston boundary
Calweton 1380
Carlton, 1547
Carlton Farm 1758
Charity Farm Bridge, current
Cherchetuna 1066
Church Lane current
Cola, Saxon personal-name
Collimer, Upper, Middle, Lower 1839
Collimer Point current
Collingwere c.1380
Colton, current
Colton Creek, current, Shotley/Chelmondiston boundary
The Downes 1839
Fletismewth (various spellings) surname fourteenth century
Great Harlings 1839
The Hanging 1839, current
Hares Creek current
Harlings 1729 (a field), current housing development
The Harrow 1594-1823
Hill House current
le Inhom c.1380
Jolixnes 'in Thorpecroft' 1380
Kaketon, Robert 1380 and 1449
Kelweton 1380
Kirkolton 1756
Kirkton (Kirketon) Manor 1290
Kirton1431
Kyrketon Manor ?thirteenth century
Kyrketune 1240
Kyrkton alias Shotley
Man's Cliff current
Mann ?Saxon personal-name
Mondes 1561
Munds, Gt Munds 1839
Old Hall, medieval manor house alias Shotley Old Hall ?n.d.
Old Hall Creek, current

Old Hall Lane, (Church Lane) twentieth century
Ovyrhalle (manor) ?fourteenth century
de Peryes, Walter 1380
Scoteleia 1066
Seven Acre Hill 1839
Shotlee hamlett 1380
Shotlee, 1410
Shotley, parish name from sixteenth century
Shotley church St Mary pre-1066
Shotley Gate, current
Shotley Gate Field, Meadow, 1839
Shotley Hall Estate, current
Shotley Hall manor 1499
Shotley Low Farm 1836
Shotley Old Hall, medieval manor house, site adjacent Old Hall Grove
Shotley Over Hall Farm, current
Shotley Rose Farm, current
Sotelege 1250
Swenyehed 1380, Swineshead 1839 and 1911 ?still in use
Thirkeltun 1240
Thurketil Danish personal-name late ninth century
Thorp 1198
Thorpe Close 1624
Thurkelton 1240
Thurketelton 1380-1756
Thurkleton 1746
Thurkolton 1756
Turchetlestuna 1066
Uplands 1839

Erwarton

Aldewarthon 1209
Aldwarton, surname 1296
Aldwarton Halle 1376
Aldewartoun, surname 1280
Alwartuna 1066
Arwarton 1568, 1586
Arwarton Hall 1999 OS map
Arwarton Parish 1999 OS map

Arwerton 1610

Arworton Hall Estate 'in the parish of Arworton 1770'

Ashwelle Broc 1650

Ashwelle Brooke 1706

Aunger, surname 1327

Denewall (a lane) 1380, ?Erwarton/Harkstead parish boundary

Earwarton 1625

Edwarton 1380

Eoforweard Saxon personal-name

Erwarton 1838 parish name current

Erwarton Bay 1955 map

Erwarton church St Mary n.d.

Erwarton Creek, map 1836-38, Erwarton/Harkstead boundary

Erwarton Hall, current

Erwarton Hall Farm, current

Erwarton Street current

Erwarton Walk 1999 map

Eurewardeston 1196, 1208

Eurewardestuna 1066

Euerwarton 1254, 1302-3

Everwardeston 1226-8

Everwarton 1316, 1344

Finn(r) the Dane 1066-1068

Godelesford, surname 1380

?Godhelms Ford ?MidSax, Erwarton/Harkstead boundary

Holy Well 1770

Johnny All Alone's Creek, current maps, was Erwarton Creek

The Lounde 1594

Rat Bridge, current, Erwarton/Harkstead boundary

Ropkins Bridge 1839 (now Rat Bridge)

Shelfe Piece in Thorpe Hall Close eighteenth century

Shop Corner (hamlet) current

Thorpe Close, Croft, Meadow seventeenth/eighteenth century

Thorpe Halle 1376

Thorpe, John de 1327

Thuri, King's thegn 1066

Walton Comon seventeenth century

Walton Hamlett sixteenth century

Warren Fields 1838

Warren Lane current

Waterhouse Creek eighteenth century, current

Harkstead

Appylton surname 1475

Bavent, Roger 1206

Beaumont Hall ? sixteenth century

Brampston, surname fifteenth/sixteenth century

Brand, Danish personal-name

Brandeston ?late fourteenth century

Brandeston Hall 1338

Brandiston, surname ? thirteenth century

Brantestun, surname ? thirteenth century

Bylam Slough, current Harkstead/Chelmondiston boundary

Caketon Hall 1414

Chapel Downe 1444

Claypit Covert current

St Clement's Chapel 1528

St Clement's Chapel Graveyard (cemetery) 1585

Climes, John, late thirteenth century

Climston, Clympston 1413-1565

Crowesoke, Crowsooke, Crowshowke, Crowshook 1566-1821

Denewall (a venella) 1380 ? Harkstead/Erwarton boundary

Erwarton Creek current

Godelsford 1380, Harkstead/Erwarton boundary

?Godhelms Ford pre-1066, ?MidSax

Gravel Pitt Fields 1839-40, Harkstead/Chelmondiston boundary

Grim, Danish personal-name 1206

Grimesdon 1206

Harkstead church St Mary n.d

Harkestead Clappits 1839

The Harrow 1735

Harte, Sir Percival sixteenth century

Hereca, eighth century Saxon personal-name

Herchesteda 1066

Herkestede Marsh 1380

Kason Wood 1839

Lythwodheth 1490

Martle Bourn(e) sixteenth/seventeenth century

Mortal Bones current

Myrtle Bones 1839

Oaketon 1282

Oketon 1282

Pesel, William 1206
Pourtepet 1327
Purpette fourteenth/eighteenth century
Purpetts 1499
Purta, Saxon personal-name
Purte pyt 1066, Harkstead/Woolverstone boundary
Rat Bridge current Harkstead/Erwarton boundary
Ropkins Bridge 1839 Rat Bridge now
Sawen Oke 1582
Skaldefen 1429
Skalde Fenn Wood 1568
Wronge Oake 1568

Holbrook

?Aelflaed, Saxon personal-name
Alfildestuna 1066
?Alfhild, Scandinavian personal-name
Alton, 1275 and 1319
de Alton, William and Matthew 1327
Alton Green, current Harkstead/Holbrook boundary
Alton Hall Cottages, current
Alton Water reservoir, current
Brantham, Joan ? fourteenth century
Brantham, William held lands in Holbrook ? fourteenth century
Branthams ? fourteenth century; twentieth-century house-name
Caketon 1419
Haketon (?Kaketon), Elias de 1327
Holbrook Bay current
Holbrook church All Saints ?post-1066
Holbrook Mill current
Holbrook Park (woodland) current
Holbrook Stream current
Holebroc 1066
Holton Green 1783, Holbrook/Harkstead boundary
Kaketon, Elias de 1327
Old Alton Hall Farm current
Sondirlondes, Christina ? fourteenth century
Sondirlond, Joan, ? fourteenth century

Stutton

Appletree Field 1844
Argent Hall Farm current
Breggewode 1304
Markwall, surname 1327
Markwell's Farm current
Mondelond ?early to mid-thirteenth century
New Mill Creek current Stutton/Brantham boundary
Samford River current Stutton/Brantham boundary
Stutton Bridge current
Stutton church St Peter pre-1066
Stutton Manor thirteenth century and current
Stuttona, Stuttuna, Stotuna 1066

Places beyond the Shotley Peninsula

In Suffolk
Belstead parish
    Belstead Brook, Belstead Bridge
Bentley (?Tattingstone) parish
    Ford, later bridged at Bentley Mill
    Ford, now footbridge over Holbrook Stream, Wherstead/Bentley north of
    Hubbards Hall
Brantham parish
    Ford (Saunford) now Brantham Bridge: Samford Hundren Moot Stow
    Saunford White House (Court Farm House): later Moot Stow
Burgh
    LIA/Roman site
Capel St Mary parish
    Ford, later Lattinford Bridge, on Roman road over mill stream
    Mill Hill Roman site
Coddenham (Combretovium)
    Pre-Cunobelin coins
    Roman site
Felixstowe parish
    Domnoc/Dommoc — St Felix' see
    Filchestowe 1298
    Walton (Felixstowe) Roman fort

Felixstowe peninsula (Colneis Hundred)
    DB data
Hintlesham
    Stigand's manor (Berewick ?Chelmondiston)
Ipswich Borough
    Roman villa, Castle Hill
    Saxon town Gipeswic
    Priory of St Peter (Saints Peter and Paul)
Pakenham
    Roman site
Rendelsham
    Raedwald's 'country seat'
Stoke by Nayland
    ?Priory
Sutton Hoo
    Ship Burial
Washbrook parish
    Roman road fording Belstead Brook at Wassebrok

In Essex
Assandun
    Battle site ?Assington ?Ashton
Brightlingsea
    King Harold's manor
Colchester
    LIA settlement (Camulodunum) Roman fort and town
    Roman road Colchester to Coddenham (Combretovium)
    Port at Fingringhoe
Collins Creek, Blackwater Estuary
    Fish trap
Harwich
    Herewic, Viking camp
Kir(k)by le Soken and Thorpe le Soken
    Danish origin
Maldon
    Battle
Mistley
    Roman port and land route to Colchester

Othona
    Roman fort

Springfield Lyons
    Bronze Age and Saxon sites
Walton on the Naze
    ?Roman fort and later haven
Woodham Walter
    Iron Age site

In Cornwall
    Climston and Stoke Climsland, current

In Kent
    Dartford, Dominican Priory of Nuns fourteenth century

Sources

Documentary Sources
Berners Estate Archives: all parishes except Stutton
Manorial records
Parish Records
PCC Wills Canterbury (indexes)
Probate records: Calendar of Wills Archdeaconry of Suffolk volumes I and II
  1444-1700
Redstone Indexes
Suffolk County Council Archaeological Service Sites and Monuments Records
Tithe Apportionment Lists and Maps

Principal printed sources
Cameron, K. *English Place-Names* fourth ed (London 1988)
Copinger, W.A. *Suffolk Manors* 6 volumes (Manchester 1910)
Copinger, W.S. *Suffolk Records and MSS* (London 1904)
Dodswell, B. *Feet of Fines for the County of Suffolk in the Reign of King John* (London
  1958)
Ekwall, E. *The Oxford Dictionary of English Place-Names* fourth edition (Oxford
  1966)
Ekwall, E. *English River Names* (Oxford 1928)
English Place-Names Society Journals
Field, J. *English Field-Names: A Dictionary* (Gloucester 1989)
Field, J. *A History of English Field-Names* (London 1993)
Gelling, M. *Place-Names in the Landscape: The geographical roots of Britain's place-
  names* (London 1984)
Gelling, M. *Signposts to the Past: Place-Names and the History of England* (Chichester
  1997)
Gelling, M. and Cole, A. *The Landscape of Place-Names* (Stamford 2000)
Hervey, S.H.A. (ed.) *Suffolk in 1327 being a Subsidy Return* Green Books No ix
  (Woodbridge 1906)
Hervey, S.H.A. (ed.) *Shotley Parish Records* Green Books No xii (Bury St Edmunds
  1912)
Mills, D. *A Dictionary of English Place-Names* second edition (Oxford 1998)

Parsons, D.N. and Styles, T. *Vocabulary of English Place-Names* volume 1 1977 volume 2 2000 (Nottingham)

Proceedings of the Suffolk Institute of Archaeology and History 1833 to date

Rumble, A. (ed.) *The Domesday Survey of Suffolk* 2 volumes Latin and English (Chichester 1986)

Rye, W. *Feet of Fines for the County of Suffolk* (Ipswich 1900)

Smith, A.H. (ed.) *English Place-Name Elements Parts I and II* EPNS volumes xxv and xxvi (Cambridge 1956)

Swanton, Michael (trs and ed.) *Anglo-Saxon Chronicles* (London 2000)

Whitelock, D. (ed.) *English Historical Documents* volume 1 second edition (Oxford 1978)

Abbreviations used in the text

ARW	Erwarton (in SMR references)
ASC	Anglo-Saxon Chronicle
BAR	British Archaeological Reports
CENS	Centre for English Name Studies (Nottingham)
Ct	Court (manorial)
CBA	Council for British Archaeology
CHL	Chelmondiston
DB	Domesday Book
EAA	East Anglian Archaeology
EH	Bede: Ecclesiastical History of the English People
EPNS	English Place-Name Society
FF	Feet of Fines
FRT	Freston
Gr Bks	Green Books (Hervey)
HOL	Holbrook
HRK	Harkstead
IPM	Inquisition post mortem
LIA	Late Iron Age
n.d.	Not dated
NMR	National Monuments Records
OE	Old English
ON	Old Norse
OS	Ordnance Survey
PRO	Public Record Office
PSIA(H)	Proceedings of the Suffolk Institute of Archaeology (and History)
RB	Romano-British
SAM	Scheduled Ancient Monument
SLY	Shotley
SMR	Sites and Monuments Records (Suffolk)
STU	Stutton
SROI	Suffolk Record Office Ipswich Branch
TM	Tithe Map
VCH	Victoria County Histories
WHR	Wherstead
★	before a personal-name indicates that it is inferred from philological evidence though not recorded

Bibliography

Arnott, W.G. *The Story of the Orwell River* (Woodbridge 1954)

Baron, M.C. *A Study of the Place-Names of East Suffolk* (Unpublished MA thesis Sheffield 1952)

Bassett, S. 'In Search of the Origins of the Anglo-Saxon Kingdoms' in *The Origins of Anglo-Saxon Kingdoms* (Leicester 1989)

Beardall, C.H., Dryden, R.C., and Holze, T.J. *The Suffolk Estuaries* (Segment Publications. Marks Tey Essex 1991 p.63)

Blair, J. *Minsters and Parish Churches. The Local Church in Transition 950-1200* Oxford University Committee for Archaeology Monograph 18 (Oxford 1988)

Cameron, K. *Place-Name Evidence for the Anglo-Saxon invasion and Scandinavian Settlements. A Collection of Eight Studies* (EPNS Nottingham 1977)

Cameron, K. *English Place-Names* revised edn 1991 (London 1997)

Campbell, J. (ed.) John, E. and Wormald, P. *The Anglo-Saxons* Lavishly illustrated including 'picture essays' (London 1982 reprinted 1991)

Carver, M.O.H. (ed.) *The Age of Sutton Hoo* (Woodbridge 1992 pb 1994)

Carver, M.O.H. *Sutton Hoo: Burial Ground of Kings?* (British Museum Press London 1998)

Coates, R. and Breeze, A. *Celtic Voices, English Places* (Spalding 2000)

Darby, H.C. *The Domesday Geography of Eastern England* (Cambridge 1971 third edition)

Darby, H.C. and Versey, G.R. *Domeday Gazetteer* (Cambridge 1975)

Davis, H.R.C. 'East Anglia and the Danelaw' (*Trans. Royal Historical Society*, fifth series volume 5 1955 pp 23-40)

Dodwell, B. *Feet of Fines for the Counties of Norfolk and Suffolk in the Reign of King John 1999-1214* (Pipe Roll Society London 1959)

Ekwall, E. *English River Names* (Oxford 1928)

Ekwall, E. *The Oxford Dictionary of English Place-Names* (Oxford 1966 fourth edition)

Esmond-Cleary, C. *The ending of Roman Britain* (London 1989)

Evans, A.C. *The Sutton Hoo Ship Burial* (British Museum Press London 1994 revised edition)

Fairclough, J. and Plunkett, S.J. 'Drawings of Walton Castle and Other Monuments in Walton and Felixstowe.' Part 2: Notes on the History of Walton Castle (*Proceedings of the Suffolk Institute of Archaeology and History* volume XXXIX part 4, 2000 pp 446-459)

Fellows-Jensen, G. 'The Vikings in England. A Review' (*Anglo-Saxon England* volume 4 Cambridge 1975)

Fellows-Jensen, G. 'Place-Names and settlement history — a review with selected bibliography' (*Northern History* volume 13 3-26 1977)

Fellows-Jensen, G. *Scandinavian Names in the East Midlands* (Uppsala 1978)

Fellows-Jensen, G. 'Scandinavian Settlement Names in East Anglia; Some Problems' (*Nomina* 22 1999 pp 44-60)

Field, J. *English Field-Names: A Dictionary* (Gloucester 1972)

Field, J. *A History of English Field-Names* (London 1993)

Gelling, M. *Signposts to the Past* (Chichester 1997 third edition)

Gelling, M. *Place-Names in the Landscape* (London 1984)

Gelling, M. and Cole, A. *The Landscape of Place-Names* (Stamford 2000)

Gill, D., Plouviez, J., Symonds,R. and Tester, C. 'Roman pottery manufacture at Bourne Hill, Wherstead' (*EAA Occasional Papers* No … 2001)

Hart, C.R. *The Danelaw* (London 1992)

Hart, C.R. *Early Charters of Eastern England* (Leicester 1966)

Hervey, S.H.A. (ed.) *Shotley Parish Records* Green Books xvi volume 2 (Bury St Edmunds 1912)

Hervey, S.H.A. (ed.) *Suffolk in 1327 being a Subsidy Return* Green Books ix (Woodbridge 1906)

Hines, J. 'The Scandinavian character of Anglian England in the pre-Viking period' *BAR* 124 (Oxford 1984)

Hines, J. (ed.) *The Anglo-Saxons from the Migration Period to the Eighth Century; an ethnographic perspective* (Woodbridge 1997)

Hingley, R. *Rural Settlement in Roman Britain* (London 1989)

Hodges, R. *Dark Age Economics* (London 1982)

Hodges, R. *The Anglo-Saxon Achievement* (London 1989)

Hodskinson, J. *The County of Suffolk Surveyed, 1783* (D.P. Dymond ed. Suffolk Record Society xv 1972)

Jackson, K.H. *Language and History in Early Britain* (Edinburgh 1953)

Laverton, S. *Exploring the Past through Place-Names: Woolverstone* (Stamford 1996)

Lee, B.A. 'Introduction to the Suffolk Domesday' in *A History of Suffolk The Victoria County Histories* volume I Suffolk (London 1911)

Mack, R.P. *The coinage of ancient Britain* (London 1987)

Maitland, F.W. *Domesday and Beyond. Three Essays on the Early History of England* (Cambridge 1999 pp 45-99)

Margeson, S. *The Vikings in Norfolk* (Norfolk Museum Service 1997)

Martin, E.A. 'Suffolk in the Iron Age' in *Land of the Iceni: the Iron Age in Northern East Anglia* Davies, J. and Williamson, T. (eds) Centre for East Anglian Studies 1999 pp 45-99

Martin, E.A. 'Settlements on Hill Tops: seven pre-prehistoric sites in Suffolk' (*EAA* 65 1993)

Martin, E.A. 'Burgh: the Iron Age and Roman Earthwork' (*EAA* 40 1988)

McLynn, F. *The Year of the Three Battles* (London 1998)

Mills, A.D. *A Dictionary of English Place-Names* (Oxford 1998 second edition)

Milne, G. 'Marine Traffic between the Rhone and Roman Britain' (*CBA Research Report* 71 1990)

Morris, R. *Churches in the Landscape* (London 1989, pb 1997)

Murphy, P. 'The Anglo-Saxon landscape and rural economy: some results from sites in East Anglia and Essex' in J. Rackham 'Environment and Economy in Anglo-Saxon Britain' *CBA Research Report* 89, 1994

Nash, D. *Coinage in the Celtic World* (London 1987)

Newman, J. 'Wics, trade, and the hinterlands' in *Anglo Saxon Trading Centres beyond the Emporia* pp 32-47 (Glasgow, 1999)

Ordnance Survey Britain before the Norman Conquest, with 10m:in map (1973)

Rackham, O. *The History of the Countryside* (London 1986)

Rackham, O. *Trees and Woodland in the British Landscape* (London 1990 revised edition)

Rye, W. *A Calendar of the Feet of Fines for the County of Suffolk* (Ipswich 1900)

Rumble, A. (ed.) *The Domesday Book of Suffolk* 2 volumes (Chichester 1986)

Salway, P. *Roman Britain* (Oxford 1981 pb 1984)

Sandred, K.J. *English Place-Names in -stede* (Uppsala 1963)

Sawyer, P.H. *Anglo-Saxon charters: an annotated list and bibliography* (London 1968)

Sawyer, P.H. *The Age of the Vikings* (London 1971 second edition)

Sawyer, P.H. (ed.) *Domesday Book. A reassessment* (London 1985)

Sawyer, P.H. *From Roman Britain to Norman England* (London 1998 second edition)

Shirley-Price, L. *Ecclesiastical History of the English People*, revised Latham, R.E. (London 1990)

Simper, R. *River Orwell and River Stour* (Woodbridge 1997)

Smith, A.H. (ed.) *English Place-Name Elements* Parts I and II (Cambridge 1956)

Stenton, F.M *Anglo-Saxon England* (Oxford 1971 third edition)

Stenton, F.M. 'The historical bearing of place-name studies: the Danish settlement of eastern England' in *Trans Roy. Hist. Soc* fourth series XXIV pp 1-24 1941

Swanton, M.(trs. and ed.) *The Anglo-Saxon Chronicles* (London 2000 second edition)

Taylor, C.C. *Village and Farmstead: History of Rural Settlement in England* (London 1964 pb 1983)

The Vikings in England and in their Danish Homelands An illustrated catalogue and sixteen essays produced for the Exhibition in Copenhagen, Aarhus and York in 1981-82. (The Anglo-Danish Viking Project 1981)

von Feilitzen, O. *The pre-Conquest names of the Domesday Book* (Uppsala 1977)

Wade, K. 'The Urbanisation of East Anglia: The Ipswich Perspective' in Gardiner, J. (ed.) 'Flatlands and Wetlands: Current Themes' in *EAA* No 50 Norwich 1993 pp 144-161

Wainwright, F.T. *Archaeology and Place-Names and History; an essay on problems of coordination* (London 1962)

Walker Harold, F.W. *The Last Anglo-Saxon King* (Stroud 1997, pb 2000)

West, S.E. 'A Corpus of Anglo-Saxon Material from Suffolk' (*EAA* 84 1999)

Whitelock, D. (ed.) *English Historical Documents* volume 1 (London 1979 second edition)

Whitelock, D. 'The pre-Viking Church in East Anglia' in *Anglo-Saxon England* volume I 1972 pp 16-22

Whitelock, D. (ed.) *Anglo-Saxon Wills* (Cambridge 1930)

Williams, A. *Kingship and Government in pre-Conquest England* (London 1999)

Yorke, B. *Kings and Kingdoms in Early Anglo-Saxon England* (London 1990, reprinted 1999)

Zincke, F.B. *Wherstead* (Ipswich 1893 second edition)

References

Chapter 1

1   Simper, R. *The River Orwell and the River Stour: English Estuaries* (Woodbridge 1997)
2   *Suffolk Parish Histories: East Suffolk* Suffolk County Council volume 1 1990
3   Rackham, O. *Ancient Woodland* (London 1980) pp337-9

Chapter 2

1   Martin, E.A. 'Suffolk in the Iron Age in Land of the Iceni' *East Anglian Studies* 1999 pp 45-99. 'Settlements on Hill-tops' *EAA* 65 1993. 'Burgh: The Iron Age and Roman Earthwork' *EAA* 40 1988.
     Cunliffe, B. *Iron Age Communities* (London 1974)
2   McGrail, S. 'Boats and boatmanship in the late pre-historic southern North Sea and Channel region' *CBA Research Report* No 71 1990
3   Fairclough, J. and Plunkett, S.J. *PSIA XXXIX* Pt 4,2000 pp419-459
4   Hart, C.R. *The Danelaw* p 210
5   Bruce-Mitford, R.L.S. *The Sutton Hoo Ship Burial* volumes 1, 2, 3 1975, 1978, 1983
6   Care Evans, A. *The Sutton Hoo Ship Burial* British Museum Press (London 1994)
7   Carver, M.O.H. *Sutton Hoo: Burial Ground of Kings?* (London 1998).
8   Henig, M. *Religion in Roman Britain* (London 1984)
9   Bede EH II 15
10   West, S. 'Corpus of Anglo-Saxon Material from Suffolk' *EAA* 84 1998. Newman, J. *British Numismatic J* 65 217-8 1995
11   Rigold, S.E.J. *British Archaeology* 24 55-9 1961; ib 37 97-102 1974
12   Coates, R. 'Domnoc/Dommoc, Dunwich and Felixstowe' in *R Coates and A Breeze. Celtic Voices, English Places* (Spalding 2000)
13   Morris, R. 'The Church in British Archaeology' *CBA Research Report* No 13 1976: Churches in the Landscape (London 1989)
14   Wade, K. 'The urbanisation of East Anglia; the Ipswich perspective' in *EAA* 50 1993

15   Swanton, M. *The Anglo-Saxon Chronicle*: Winchester and Peterborough MSS 880 (879)

16   Davis, R.H.C. *Trans Roy Hist Soc* 5th series. Volume 5 1955 pp23-7; Sawyer, P.H. *The Age of the Vikings* 1971

17   *Britain before the Norman Conquest* Map 10m:in. Ordnance Survey 1973

18   Hart, C. *The Danelaw* pp25-113

19   *The Battle of Maldon: Fact or Fiction* Cooper, J. (ed.) (London 1993)

20   *Anglo-Saxon Chronicle* A, D, C 1016

21   *The Domesday Book of Suffolk*

Chapter 3

1   PPG 16 Planning Policy Guidance. Department of the Environment November 1990

2   Newman, J. *The Late Roman and Anglo-Saxon Settlement Pattern in the Sandlings of Suffolk in The Age of Sutton Hoo* (Woodbridge 1992)
     Margeson, S. *The Vikings in Norfolk* (Norwich 1997)
     Glazebrook, J. (ed.) *EAA* Occasional Papers: Research and Archaeology: Framework for the Eastern Counties. 1. Resource Assessment 1997

3   Blinkhorn, P. *The Ipswich-Ware Project: Pilot Survey* (Northampton County Council 1994)

4   Murphy, P. 'The Anglo-Saxon landscape and rural economy: some results from sites in East Anglia and Essex'. *CBA Research Report* 89 1994 pp23-39

Chapter 4

1   Dodgson, J.McN. 'The significance of the distribution of English place-names in…-ingas, -inga in south-east England.' *J Medieval Archaeology* X 1-29, 1966

2   Cox, B. 'The Place-Names of the Earliest English Records'. *EPNSJ* 8 1974/5 pp12-66

3   Gelling, M. *Signposts to the Past* (Chichester 1997)

4   Gelling, M. *Place-Names in the Landscape* (London 1984)

5   Gelling, M. and Cole, A. *The Landscape of Place-Names* (Stamford 2000)

Chapter 5

1   Bede: EH III 22

2   Stoke Charter CS 1269:8 AD 970: boundary clause. Trans Hart, C. in *The Danelaw* 1992 pp60-62

3   Whitelock, D. (ed.) *Anglo-Saxon Wills* xv (Cambridge 1930)
4   Rumble, A (ed.) *Domesday Book Suffolk* 2 vols Chichester 1986 Latin with English translation

Chapter 6
1   Thomas, R. *Oxford J Arch.* 16(2) 211-16 1997
2   Hingley, R. *Rural Settlement in Roman Britain* (London 1989)
3   Gregory, T. and Rogerson, A. *EAA* 54 1992 69-72
4   Smith I 8 and 58
5   Laverton, S. *Exploring the Past through Place-Names; Woolverstone* (Stamford 1995) pp79 and 91
6   Smith I 185, II 244
7   Wolverston Manor Ct 32Eliz.S1/10/5.1
8   Reymes deeds HD 210 1/91, 1/122 ib 1/84, 1/91, 1/164; Erwarton Court Book 1663 S1/10/81 1-2
9   Smith II 135
10   Hervey, S.H.A. (ed.) *Shotley Parish Records* Suffolk Gr Bks xvi vol 2 Bury St Edmunds p 269
11   Smith I 28
12   Smith I 274 II 33, 63
13   Field, J A *History of English Field-Names* (London 1993) pp 216-7
14   Gill, D., Plouviez J., Symonds, R.P. and Tester, C. 'Roman pottery manufacture at Bourne Hill, Wherstead.' *East Anglian Occasional Paper* 2001
15   Buckley, D.G. and Hedge, J.D. 'The Bronze Age and Saxon Settlements at Springfield Lyons, Essex: An Interim Report.' *Essex County Council Occasional Papers 5* 1987
16   Zincke, F.B. *Wherstead* (Ipswich second edn 1893)
17   Smith I 54
18   Bacon's Annals of Ipswich 1654 pp 1.2; Perambulation of the Bounds of the Borough of Ipswich 1352(sic); Perambulation of the Bounds of Ipswich 1351, in Ipswich Borough Archives C/135/4
19   Webb, J. 'The Great Tooley of Ipswich' Appendix B pp165-67; *Notes on Tooley's Accounts Book 1538* (Suffolk Record Society Ipswich 1962)
20   Arnott, W.G. *The Story of the Orwell River* (Woodbridge 1954)
21   Gelling, M. *Place-Names in the Landscape* pp41-50
22   Smith II 272 and 147
23   Gelling, M. and Cole, A. *The Landscape of Place-Names* p 68
24   A Plan of Thorington estate in 1676 (SROI X6/9)
25   Field, J. *The History of English Field-Names* (London 1993 p212)
26   Schedule of Berners Estate Lands 1830. S1/10/4/1

27   de Jersey, P. and Newman, J. *British Numismatic J* volume 6 pp.214-16 1995

28   Scott, V.M. *Stutton Local History Group Journal* No 3 April 1985

29   *V C H Suffolk* volume i 309; PSIA I 1841 p151

Chapter 7

1   Plouviez, J. in *Roman Small Towns in Eastern England and Beyond*. Brown, A.E. (ed.) Oxbow Monographs 52 1995; and Plouviez, J. forthcoming.

2   Hines, J. 'The Scandinavian character of Anglian England in the pre-Viking period'. *Brit. Arch. Res. Rep.* 124, 1984

3   Hines, J. (ed.) 'The Anglo-Saxons from the Migration Period to the Eighth Century'. *Papers and discussions at the second symposium on the Anglo-Saxons, San Merino*. (Woodbridge 1997)

Chapter 8

1   Margeson, S. *The Vikings in Norfolk* (Norwich 1997)

2   The Mills Manuscripts held in Stutton by the Local History Group

3   *PSIA* vol 33 1976 p102

4   Rackham, *O. Ancient Woodland: its history, vegetation, and uses in England* (London 1980 pp 337-38)

Chapter 9

1   Cox, B.H. *JEPNS* vol. 5 1972 pp15-78

2   Cox, B.H. *JEPNS* vol. 8 1974-5 pp12-55

3   Smith II 147-9; Sandred, K.I. *English place-names in -stede* (Uppsala 1963)

4   HD 210 1/180

5   Harkstead Manor Ct 6HenV S1/10/6.1

6   Harkstead Manor Ct Rolls 1413-1657 S1/10/6.1-6.5; English abstract 52/16/14.7; Accounts Roll 1419-80 S1/10/6.6

7   Gover, J.E.B. *Place-Names of Cornwall*. Unpublished typescript held in the Cornish Record Office Truro

8   Smith I 59

9   HD 210 1/108

10   Ipswich Portmanmote Rolls 1280-1282 C/2/1/1/6-7 *Ipswich Borough Archives 1255-1835: A Catalogue*. Allen, D. (ed.) (Woodbridge 2000)

11   HD 210 1/150

12   HD 210 3 /1 Will Robert de Reymes

13   Holbrook Ct Roll 1378-1399 S1/10/9

14   Smith I 257

15   Smith I 79

16   Smith I 138

17   Laverton, S. *Exploring the Past through Place-Names: Woolverstone* (Stamford 1995 p 79)

18   Gelling, M. *Place-Names in the Landscape* 1984 p245

19   Wolverston Manor Ct 12HenVIII S1/10/5.1

20   Smith I 152 II 113

21   Wolverston Manor Ct 32Eliz in S1/10/5.1

22   Smith II 97

23   IPM Elizabeth Wolverston PRO C.138/40/1 trs Hervey Gr Bks xvi volume 2

24   Inquisition Richard Wolverston PRO C 142/31/6

25   S1/10/4.9

26   Gelling, M. and Cole, A. *The Landscape of Place-Names* p200

27   Dymond, D. and Virgoe, R. *PSIA* XXXVI pt 2 p94

28   Harkstead Manor Ct S1/10/6.2 14EdIV 1475

29   HD 32 283/168

30   Rye, W. FF 10EdI 1282

31   Harkstead Manor Ct 24Eliz S1/10/6.3

32   Smith II 107-8

33   Gr Bks ix (2)

34   Harkstead Manor Ct Records S1/10/6.1-6.5: English Abstract GC15: 52316/14.7

35   Will William Tenderyng 1501 PRO PROB 11/12

36   Reymes Deeds HD 210

37   Baron, C. unpublished MA thesis Sheffield 1952 TS s924.4 in SROI

38   Smith II 255

39   *Essex Archaeology* 1998 p1 (Essex County Council); *British Archaeology* No 41 1999 p5

40   Reymes Deeds HD 210

41   Sandred, K.I. *English Place-Names in -stede* (Uppsala 1963)

42   HD 210 1/2 n.d. ?thirteenth century

43   HD 210 1/171 n.d. ?thirteenth century

44   Rye, W. FF 11EdIII 1338; VCH Kent vol 2 p 182 footnote 19

45   Will Sir Percival Harte PRO C 66/689 1580

46   Tanner Index of Institution Books vol ii Samford Deanery NRO

47   Rye, W. FF 10John 1209; HD 210/1/82 1280; HD 210/1/88 1296

48   IPM Sir Bartholemew Bacon 15RichII abstr. in Cal. IPM Brit Rec Soc 1824 vol III

49   Ordnance Survey Map 2in:m Explorer 197. 1999

50   Smith I 8 II 247

51   Erwarton Ct Bks S1/10/8.1 and 8.2 1637-1708

52   Dodnash Priory Charters. Suffolk Charters XVI Harper-Bill, C. (ed.) Suffolk Record Society (Woodbridge 1998)

53   Copinger, W.A., *Suffolk Manors* Hervey Gr Bks ix vol 2

54   Wolverston Manor Ct Roll S1/10/5.1 22EdIII

55   IPM Elizabeth Wolverston 1419 PRO C. 138/40/1; trs Gr Bks xvi (2)

56   Harkstead Ct Roll 3HenV S1/10/6.1

57   HD 210 1/4, 5,6

58   Holbrook Subsidy Return 1327 trs Gr Bks ix

59   Rental Kirkton Manor 1380 Gr Bks xvi (2)

60   Quitclaim Gr Bks xvi (2)

61   HD 210 1/187

62   HD 210 1/84, 86, 127, 130, 164

63   HD 670/16 Extent and Survey of the Manors of Wherstead Hall Bourne Hall and Pannington Hall with rentals 1700; Reymes Deeds HD 210 1/82-164

64   Gr Bks xvi (2)

65   Rye, W. FF 13EdI 19

66   HD 11 52/1, 2

67   HB 54:4560

68   1in:m OS map first edition revised 1836-38. David and Charles edition 1970

69   *The Woolverstone Estate: Particulars and Plans* John D Wood and Co Auctioneers July 1958

Chapter 10

1   Smith I 95

2   Kirkton Manor Rental 1380 Gr Bks xvi vol 2

3   Rye, W. FF 10RichI 56; Gr Bks xvi vol 2

4   IPM Sir Henry Felton 1ChasI; Gr Bks xvi vol 2

5   Erwarton Subsidy Return Gr Bks ix

6   IPM Sir Bartholemew Bacon 15RichII; abstract in Cal. IPM Brit. Rec. Soc. 1821 vol III

7   Erwarton Ct Books 1626-83 and 1691-1708 S1/10/8.1-2; Erwarton Ct Roll 1691-1708 S1/10/8.7; Evidence of Title 1691-1708 S1/10/8.101

8   Smith II 247

9   Harkstead Manor Cts 18EdV S1/10/6.2 and 10Eliz S1/10/6.3

10   Kirkton Manor rental 1380 Gr Bks xvi vol 2

11   Smith II 244 I 129

12   Beardall, C.H., Dryden, R.C. and Holzer, T.J. *The Suffolk Estuaries* (Segment Publications Marks Tey Essex 1991) p63

13   Harkstead Manor Accounts Roll S1/10/6.6 26-27HenVI

14   Dodwell, B. (ed.) *Feet of Fines of the County of Suffolk in the reign of King John* (Pipe Roll Society 1956) p225

15   S1/10/10.7

16   Smith I 210; Gelling, M. *Signposts to the Past* 1997 pp 148-49; 158-61

17   Weldon Finn, R. *Domesday Studies: The Eastern Counties* (London 1867) pp7, 22, 210

18   Fellows-Jensen, G. in *The Reign of King Cnut, King of England, Denmark and Norway 1016-35*. Rumble, A. (ed.) (London 1994)

19   Smith II 3

20   Smith II 247

21   Will John Elys Harkstead R10/75 1528; Will Roger Andrews alias Peynter sailor Harkstead R32/331 1585

22   Vocabulary of English Place-Names Á-Box 1997 Centre for English Name Studies Nottingham; Smith I 59

23   Smith I 39

24   Smith I 196

25   Smith II 233

Chapter 11

1   *An Historical Atlas of Suffolk* Dymond, D. and Martin, E. (eds) 3rd edn 1999 Suffolk County Council

2   Bryant's Map of Suffolk 1826. S192 BRY in SROI

3   Stenton, F.W. *Anglo-Saxon England* 3rd edn Oxford 1971 p279; Maitland, F.W. *Domesday Book and Beyond* Essay III: The Hide 1987 edn Cambridge; Anderson-Ansgart, O. *The English Hundred Names* (Lund 1934)

4   Wherstead Manor Extent 1700 HD 670/16 fo.11v

5   Dodnash Priory Charter No 196, Suffolk Charters XVI Christopher Harper-Bill (ed.) Suffolk Record Society (Woodbridge 1998)

6   Will 1312 Robert de Reymes HD 210 3/1

7   Hart, C.R. *The Danelaw* 1992 p61; Reymes Deeds HD 210

8   Will Edmund Legy, Wherstead IC/AA1/28

9   Hart, C.R. *The Early Charters of Eastern England* (Leicester 1966) p59

10   Kirkton Manor Rental 1380 in Gr Bks xvi (2)

11   McGrail, S. (ed.) 'Maritime Celts, Frisians and Saxons' *CBA Research Report* No 71 1990; McGrail, S. *Studies in Marine Archaeology*. BAR British Series No 256 (Oxford 1997); Marsden, P. *Ships and Shipwrecks* (London 1997)

12   Going, G. 'The Roman Countryside' p95 and Fig1.G in *The Archaeology of Essex. Proceedings of the 1993 Writtle Conference* Bedwin, O. (ed.) (Chelmsford 1996)

13   Moir, R. and Maynard, G. *PSIA* XXI 240-62, 1933; Moore, I.E. ib. XXIV 168-181, 1948; *Ipswich Archaeological Trust Newsletter* No 48 1997

14   *Essex Domesday Book* ii f 5b6a

15   Smith I 239

16   Bond Hall Estate, Freston: Map 1774 HA 93 887/5; Freston Tithe Map 1841

17   Wolverston Manor Ct Rolls S1/10/5.1; Laverton, S. *Exploring the Past through Place-Names: Woolverstone* (Stamford 1995)

18   HB 54:4560 Indenture conveying land in Chelmondiston

19   Smith II 27-8

20   S1/10/1.1(1)

21   Mortgage 1640 Freston Manor Hall Farm HD 22

22   Smith I 216

23   Map HE3/424 Lady Chedworth's Estate: Arwarton Hall 1770 in SROI

24   Taylor, S. *The History and Antiquities of Harwich and Dovercourt* (London 1731)

25   Gr Bks xii vol 2 p26

26   Dickens, B. in EPNS XI Surrey pp 403-6

27   Zincke, F.B. *Wherstead* 2nd edn 1893 p337

28   Stenton, F.M. *Anglo-Saxon England* (Oxford 1971 third edition). Williams, H. *Kingship and Government in pre-Conquest England* (London 1999)

29   Plan X6/9: lands and yards of Thorington Hall 1676

30   Paul Estate Wherstead Cropping Plan 1968/9

31   HD 1538/420/1 n.d. ?later twelfth-century Feoffment: Gerard de Penitun to William son of Edmund

32   W Rye FF 7RichIII: William, Prior of St Peter Ipswich, acquired land in Panington

33   Stowe Charter 410 temp HenIII i.e. 1216-1272: Gilbert, Prior of St Peter Ipswich, to Gilbert son of Robert de Reymes of Wherstead

34   HD 210 1/64 30 September 1358

35   Stowe Charter 409 1282

36   Baron,C. Wherstead Hall Manor Ct Baron 4 June 23GeoIII 1750 in unpublished MA thesis Sheffield 1952 TS s924.4 in SROI

Chapter 12

1   Rackham, O. *Trees and Woodland in the British Landscape*. 1990, revised edition pp48-51

2   Rackham, O. ib. and *Ancient Woodland* 1980 337-8

3   Maps in ASC Swanton (London 2000)

4   Walker, I. N. *Harold. The last Anglo-Saxon King* (Stroud 1997) pb 2000

Chapter 13

1   Rental of the Lord King for Saunford HA 246/D/2 n.d. ?thirteenth century in SROI

Chapter 14

1   *Sites and Monuments Records for Shotley Peninsula c.100 BC to AD 1066.* Suffolk Archaeological Service, Bury St Edmunds

Chapter 15

1   Ekwall, E. *English River Names* 1928; Baron, C. unpublished MA thesis 1953 TS qS929.4 SROI

2   Jackson, K. *Language and History in Early Britain* (Edinburgh 1953)

3   Smith II 165

4   Maps of Suffolk: Saxton 1585; Speed 1610; Ordnance Survey 1st edn revised 1836-38, David and Charles edition 1970

Index